"Beth Lisick's kaleidoscopic whirlwind tour through her secret shames is the ultimate joyride for those of us who enjoy cringe-worthy embarrassment, genuine pathos, and an overdosing amount of schadenfreude."—Michael Ian Black, comedian and author of *You're Not Doing It Right*

"This book is fucking great. There is a story in it called 'PANDA AMBULANCE!!!' How is Beth Lisick not as famous as David Sedaris?"—Kathleen Hanna, musician and activist

"These short pieces, which at first seem casually constructed and connected, are immediately funny, ironic, personable, embarrassing and oddly appealing. Yet quickly they accumulate into deep emotional resonance. Just a few pages in and I was totally involved with the struggles of this clearly talented, hilariously confused person to be better in her own weird antic backassward ways. Full of indelible phrases (Panda Ambulance!) and painfully irrefutable observations about art, crappy jobs, friendship, wealth, sex, hygiene, booze, motherhood, and so many other things, this book is basically the inverse of those sappy self-discovery memoirs that inevitably arc into hard earned wisdom and self-discovery. This writer has the courage to stay in difficult places, and therefore be truer to life. I laughed and cringed and cared more and more. Thank you, Beth Lisick, it was and continues to be worth all the struggles."—Matthew Zapruder, author of *Come On All You Ghosts*

"*Yokohama Threeway* by Beth Lisick is a whip-smart, occasionally profound, often profane, always very funny collection of somewhere around three hundred (judged by weight) short, sharp, sweet literary shocks. Speaking as someone who hates everything, I love this book."—James Greer, musician & author of *The Failure*

"What to call Beth Lisick's *Yokohama Threeway*? Part flash fiction, part poetry, part outsider art. Reality television, minus the cameras. Spoon River Anthology meets Tom Waits. I'll settle for hilarious, heartbreaking, compassionate, pitch perfect, utterly original."—Joyce Maynard, author of *After Her* and *Labor Day*

"No matter how civilized we all like to pretend we are, Lisick's writing reminds us how simultaneously wonderful and terrible it is to be alive. By baring her own 'Oh, no!' experiences, she shows us there is no shame in being human. Okay, a lot of shame. But at least it's funny shame."—Kim Wong Keltner, author of *Tiger Babies Strike Back*

Yokohama Threeway

Yokohama Threeway
AND OTHER SMALL SHAMES

Beth Lisick

City Lights Books | San Francisco

Cover illustration by David L. Cooper

Library of Congress Cataloging-in-Publication Data
Lisick, Beth, 1968–
Yokohama threeway : and other small shames / Beth Lisick.
    page cm
ISBN 978-0-87286-625-6 (pbk.)
1. Lisick, Beth, 1968—Anecdotes. 2. Authors, American—20th century—
Anecdotes. I. Title.

PS3562.I77Z479 2013
818'.5409—dc23
[B]

                                          2013020603

City Lights Books are published at the City Lights Bookstore,
261 Columbus Avenue, San Francisco, CA 94133.
www.citylights.com

Acknowledgments

Thank you Michelle Tea for all the inspiration and support over the years. You've helped many of us keep going and your faith in this book and editorial advice are huge. Thank you to this book's co-editor Elaine Katzenberger for her wisdom, plus Peter, Stacey, Robert, Jolene, and all the City Lights crew.

Sister Spit, RADAR and the organizers and fellow writers at the RADAR residency, Creative Work Fund, the artists and staff at Creativity Explored, Daniel Greenberg and Tim Wojcik of the Levine Greenberg Literary Agency, plus true pals Alan Black, Marc Capelle, Angela Coon, Tara Jepsen, Arline Klatte, Jan Richman, and Amy Sullivan.

My parents, brothers, Lora, and Penelope, always.

My kid Gus and husband Eli, forevs.

Contents

False Imprisonment

LET'S GO AROUND TO THE SIDE OF THE house. Let's do it back there. It's only piles of dirt and pool equipment and a patch of mustard greens that my brother planted. The greens were too bitter for anyone to eat and now they're dead anyway. I think that tree in the corner will be strong enough to hold her if we tie the rope tight enough. Did you get the rope from the garage? Good. She's tiny, it won't take much. Okay, now you hide behind the gate so when she opens it she won't know you're here. I'll try to get her to go over near the tree, and that's your cue to come out. Once she sees you, just keep moving toward her until we have her backed up against the tree, and then we'll tie her up tight. Wait! We need a scarf to tie around her mouth so no one can hear her scream. Go get one from my mom's closet. Hurry! There's one with colored polka dots. Now, she's going to cross Titus Avenue, coming from her dirty house that always smells like syrup where the sad, fat mom is trying to raise five kids after the dad left her for someone else who we've never seen. He thinks he's so great, that divorced Dad, in his green Audi Fox. With his golf clubs and tennis racket and bald head. You know the mom went and got super into Jesus, and now they all go to that weird huge church on the other end of the valley that people call a superchurch. All of the kids go and sing to Jesus, except for the redhead brother who is mean, mean, mean. Shannon is the best one of the kids, but we're going to tie her up anyway. She's the skinny twin, the one that popped out second, the cute one who doesn't stutter and can do good cartwheels. Why does looking through a knothole in a fence always make my eye burn? Here she comes. She's coming! Get the rope! She'll stay tied up to this tree until everyone is worried about her, whenever that happens, and she will cry and she will pay. No one warps my *Grease* soundtrack album and gets away with it.

Guitar Lessons

MY EX-BOYFRIEND'S ROOMMATE WAS GOING TO TEACH ME how to play my new guitar for ten bucks a lesson. The first few went okay. I would strap the case on my back and ride my mountain bike over the flat streets of Santa Cruz's west side, work my way through the tangle of vines at the front walk, lean the bike against the blue stucco wall, and ring the bell at 10 a.m. sharp. Ted was sweet. He would get me a glass of water or a cup of tea and we would sit in the living room, strumming chords and sometimes trying to sing. I was slightly relieved when the other roommate wasn't there. His name was Clover and he made his living by traveling to fairs and festivals, demonstrating and selling his special patented "meditation workout sticks" that were kind of like a combination of hippie devil sticks and a hackey sack. Clover bragged too much about how deeply he understood dolphins, and his hugs were always too long.

On the day I went for my fourth lesson, I rang the bell but no one answered. There was a side gate that we sometimes used when they had potlucks, so I rolled my bike into the backyard and knocked on the sliding glass door. Nothing. I slid it open a crack. The smell of nag champa and mildew was familiar. Everyone in this house, and many others around town, probably mine, smelled exactly like this. Plus a hint of cumin.

"Hello?" I called.

"Come in!" Ted yelled from the living room, the room that was directly on the other side of the front door I had just knocked on.

I walked through the kitchen and when I crossed the threshold

I was greeted by Ted's Lycra-encased package as he performed a stretch on his back, one knee to his chest and the other leg splayed out to the side.

"I'm just finishing my stretches!" he said cheerily as he hugged his knee more tightly.

Seriously? He had put on a pair of Lycra tights with nothing underneath or over them and just happened to:

1) not hear my first knock
2) have his balls and dick *facing me* as I walked into the room
3) be so involved in his routine that he couldn't stop stretching once I came in.

Also, he was approximately fifteen years older than me. Which didn't help.

He disengaged from this position, and just when I thought he was going to get up, he switched sides and pulled the opposite knee to his chest.

"I'm getting some water," I said. I had already turned my back and was on the way to the kitchen.

"Oh! Would you mind getting me some?"

I filled up two jelly jars from the tap and brought them back into the room. He got up and pulled on a pair of sweatpants.

"I thought we'd practice in my room today," he said. "I think Clover is having some friends over for brunch."

I brought my guitar into his bedroom, which was really only just big enough for his bed and one of the dining room chairs. We sat knee to knee, Ted on the bed and me on the chair, trying to work our way through Neil Young's "Helpless" again. Then I handed him the ten from my pocket and I knew it was over.

I didn't say anything to him at the time except thanks and see you next week, but when the next week rolled around and I hadn't practiced what I was supposed to, it seemed tied up with the way I felt when I imagined him correcting my fingering again. I fabricated some excuse about my work schedule, and no, I didn't need a make-up lesson, I would just catch him the following week. The following week, I was a no-show. He called me a few times, left messages on my machine, which I ignored. Whenever I ran into him after that, at the health food store or the bakery, I apologized like it was all my fault. I'm such a flake.

Dicks

MY BROTHER PAUL WAS A SENIOR WHEN I was a freshman. We hardly ever saw each other during the school day, but there were occasions when I would clock his trademark limp as he walked across the quad. Right foot leading, left food lagging. Sometimes he would do this little galloping step and start clapping his hands really fast. He had cerebral palsy, a physical disability that affected all the muscles on his left side, but he also had something else we didn't have a name for. What is it called when you memorize the *TV Guide?*

A bunch of times that year I saw this group of popular boys, lunky jocks, not the runners but maybe the baseball or football guys, making fun of him behind his back. Imitating his walk. They'd really crack themselves up and then yell something at him like *retard* or *mental case.* Or sometimes it was a question. *What's the square root of pi, retard?* He'd ignore them instead of saying 1.77245385091 like he did at home, and get into our mom's station wagon while I went to track practice.

One day, I stomped over to those jocks in my black boots with my thrift-store dog tags jangling around my neck.

No, I didn't. That would be the version where I'm some kind of cool girl hero. What actually happened is that I heard them yelling at him and my ears got hot and I never said anything to them. Not even once that whole year.

Engagement Party

I USED TO IGNORE KIDS. FROM ABOUT THE time I stopped baby-sitting at sixteen until I gave birth to one of my own, I had absolutely no interest in children whatsoever. It wasn't that I didn't like them, it's just that they didn't seem very interesting. Dogs I would pet, or occasionally pepper with direct questions, and I don't even like dogs. With kids, I saw them with my eyes and then made a decision to treat them as if they were invisible.

It was 1998 and I was at an engagement party for a woman I barely knew. I had never been to an engagement party, nor did I think people even had those anymore, and come to think of it, I haven't been to one since, so maybe they didn't and don't. My boyfriend had been invited as well, but he wouldn't be attending because he'd already learned a lesson that I wouldn't for years: you're not required to go to every party you're invited to. So I went by myself, hungover in a decent-looking sweater.

Sometimes it's fun to know no one at a party — some other high school's kegger or an asshole's blowout in a posh hotel — but a casual champagne engagement brunch in someone's apartment on a Sunday morning isn't one of them. I was among the first to arrive, and when the bride-to-be told me she loved her new neighborhood because of the "cute little bagel place around the corner," which I had always thought of as "a bagel shop," I realized this was going to be harder than I'd anticipated. There was a small stool wedged between a bookshelf and a sideboard, and that's where I planted myself, guzzling black coffee and eating whatever was within arm's reach while a parade of asses swiveled in front of my face. Socially challenging, but manageable. Then the kids arrived.

It seemed like there were twenty of them, though realistically there were probably three or four. They stomped through the place with their sticky starfish hands, dragging dirty plastic shit behind them like sea trawlers expecting special treatment. The thing about a lot of kids this age, five or six years old, is that they assume any adult is going to respond to them like their parents do. They demand favors of you or say something silly and hold for laughter like comedians. I wasn't into it. I was just waiting until it seemed like I had been there a decent amount of time and then I was going to slip out unnoticed.

The oldest boy, a blond kid in a red Izod shirt — which bothered me, a toddler Lacoste — approached and said something, I don't know what. I responded by looking right through him, which I remembered to enjoy because that's impossible to do with adults. Then he said something in his Rod and Todd Flanders voice, and I snapped to.

"Why are you wearing a wig?"

At that time in my life I was sporting the dumbest hairstyle I have ever had, which is saying quite a bit when you've been through both the Dorothy Hamill and the poodle perm. There was a salon in the Mission that was hot-gluing multicolored fake hair onto everyone's heads and they were giving a lot of treatments away for free in order to spread the gospel of this awesome new way to express yourself. This is technically what a hair extension is, right? Fake hair added to your real hair to create volume, color variables, and the look and feel of a cheap doll.

I pulled on the fake bits for him. "It's not a wig, see?" I said with a swatch of platinum acrylic "hair" between my fingers. "It's attached to my head." It wasn't lost on me that he'd turned me into a performing monkey in no time.

"It's a wig," he insisted. "Why are you wearing a wig?"

"I'm not wearing—" I caught myself. Why was I talking to a kid? Clearly, if there was ever going to be a cue to put on the vanishing cream, this was it.

I got up from my stool, and the boy started chanting, "Take off your wig, you man! Take off your wig, you man!"

There was some initial delight by the adults. A boy is singing something! What is he singing at that hungover woman with the poppyseeds in her teeth?

"Take off your wig, you man!" I started for the door, which apparently was the cue for his friends to join in. Take off your wig, you man! they chanted. Take off your wig, you man!

I walked through the small apartment with the kids following me, pied piper style, still chanting. Take off your wig, you man. Take off your wig, you man. Take off your wig . . .

I shut the door behind me, leaving my coat on the bed, and never went back to get it.

. . . you man!

How I Remember the Speech Going

HI, EVERYBODY! IT'S REALLY, UH, COOL of my brother to ask me to give the best man speech at the wedding because actually, and this is kind of weird, but people mistake me for a man sometimes. I'm not really sure why. I guess I can look kind of mannish in a way, but I also think I must have a lot of testosterone in my body and people can, like, smell it or sense it and then that's why they call me a man. I seriously have been asked if I'm in the wrong bathroom! Anyway, it's super exciting to be here at Chris and Lora's wedding. I just had a baby a few months ago and— Hey! See, I'm not a man! I had a baby! Anyway, he's a terrible sleeper, maybe you heard him screaming at the ceremony, and I'm kind of jet-lagged so I feel a little crazy right now. We left our son with some Tibetan lady who seemed really peaceful and calming so we're hoping for the best. I don't know if they found her on Craigslist or what. Whoa, what if we get out of here and we don't have a baby anymore? Maybe that wouldn't be so bad. Ha, ha. So anyway . . . Chris! He's so great, right? I don't want to embarrass him, but he has done some crazy stuff. Chris, remember when you had to borrow my truck and drive it to Reno because you were going to try to make your rent by gambling? Or when you sold the Honda that belonged to both of us and then bought an Alfa Romeo that you couldn't afford, and then I didn't have a car anymore? Oh, man. That sucked. I was like, "What?" I was all, "Dude, that car belonged to both of us and you didn't have the right to sell it!" Anyway, um, yeah! You're a great brother, though. Chris didn't have his first girlfriend until he was in high school. He's had some nice girlfriends since then, but Lora is the best! She is, like, a fully developed person who can take care of herself. Not like a few people . . . anyway! I love you guys. I love that you're having your wedding in such a classy place and you're paying for it yourselves. Are you paying for it yourselves? I think I heard that from someone in the limo, and it's so awesome if you are because people usually have to get their parents to pay for everything. Or maybe because a lot of people are getting married when they're older now they're paying for it themselves? Was there an article about that in the *Times* that I missed? About how people do that now? Oh, I'm so tired. Congratulations!

The Great Debate

IN SEVENTH GRADE WE HAD TO STAGE A debate about euthanasia and the right to die. We learned about Karen Ann Quinlan, a twenty-one-year-old woman who had fallen into a coma after coming home from a party where she reportedly drank alcohol and took a Valium after being on a crash diet. When the paramedics arrived, she was unresponsive and remained in a persistent vegetative state at the hospital. Even though her parents were devoutly Catholic, they consulted with their church and decided the respirator was "extraordinary means" and it was within the confines of their faith to remove it and allow her to return to her "natural state." The hospital, threatened with homicide charges from the county, refused, and an epic legal battle unfolded. Nearly a year later, when the court ruled in her parents' favor, the respirator was removed. Surprisingly, Karen Ann actually stayed alive, requiring only intravenous feeding. Though she eventually died of complications from pneumonia nine years later, having never regained consciousness, at the time of our junior high debate, Karen Ann was still alive.

I was fascinated by this story. Unable to grasp the more complicated issues of moral theology, the disambiguation of bioethics and the Hippocratic oath, I wanted to know about the party. What was she wearing? What was Valium and how did it make you feel? Did she have a boyfriend? Why was it called a "crash" diet? A lot of the students in my class were very adamant about what side they were on. As usual, I found it difficult to be very adamant about anything. It seemed to me if her parents were okay with letting her go, then everybody should be cool with that, right? Do the doctors or the judges or the Pope really care that much? But then again, they have rules they're supposed to follow, so there's that I guess. While kids flocked to opposite sides of the classroom to show their allegiance, I hesitated. And then I was assigned to be anti-euthanasia because that side had fewer people.

It became clear right away that I was with all the religious kids. "God gives you life and only God can take it away!" was our team's preeminent argument. After some cursory research with the encyclopedias in the library, it was showtime. A few kids were in charge of the God argument, a few more were doing the Hippocratic oath, and a group had taken on the legal ramifications. The rest of us stragglers were forced to take whatever crumb-arguments were left over.

As the debate began, I found myself moved by the position of the other team. What does it mean to be alive? What about the suffering of those who are left to take care of their comatose loved ones? Ever heard of something called the separation of church and state? And their passion! They were so much more emotionally moving than my team, who sounded like a bunch of robots, thanks mostly to our team captain Scott Winslow in his Members Only jacket and puka shell necklace.

Our team was clearly losing. All our strongest arguments had already been made when Scott looked over to me to see if we could pull it out at the last minute. Inspired by the raw emotion I'd seen on the other side, I took my paper to the podium and tried to emulate that fire. With a voice full of conviction I read the only words I had written down.

"What about quantity over quality?!"

There was a brief pause as I realized I was now expected to back that up with a persuasive speech.

"Maybe what matters in life is how long you live!" I began. "Maybe it's better if you can live to be a hundred because even if you're on life support you are still technically alive if your heart is beating!" Even as I was saying it, I knew how stupid it sounded. Everybody knew. Kids on the other team laughed. Even the teacher looked incredulous. Quantity over quality in a debate about life.

I was now watching myself from the outside as I retreated against the chalkboard as the verdict came in. We had lost in a landslide. No one from the visiting class had voted for us. The winning team hugged each other and high-fived, fully stoked in a teenage way, but they also seemed older, cooler. We had been babies spitting out what our parents or churches had taught us while they had a deep understanding and world-weariness about having to pull the plug on a life sometimes. I didn't like where I was. I needed to figure out what it took to get over to the other side.

It's Date Night, Francis

SEVEN GLASSES OF A PEPPERY PINOT GRIGIO PASS by on a silver tray. From the corner I watch that girl with the eczema and far-apart eyes smell her armpit when she doesn't think anyone is looking. Her eyes flit over to mine, catching me catching her as the wings of my heart morph into hands and burst into applause. I've been working on my faces, and I hope the expression I'm making right now is saying exactly this:

> *Why, hello. I remember you from various dark bars in the '90s. Will you now join my secret society? All you have to do is never pretend we're all not really related to monkeys. Let's start something. Wait, I forget, is your name Tammy?*

The chill in the air is different from the legendary foggy chill of the coldest winter ever spent in summer. It is a slap of bracing sea air, blowing in off the bay and hitting me hard tonight. Date Night. When else but Date Night can you come home to find a Craigslist teen babysitter asleep on your couch with the heat blasting and the TV on, and then pay her a bunch of money you'd rather be spending on a cleaning lady or getting that wart removed from your left nostril?

Has your marriage shit the bed? Try Date Night!

In high school, eating a smashed sandwich in the portable trailer that was our journalism classroom, I had dreamed of one day attending a party like this. The golden glow of early evening, a party celebrating the publication of an obscure quarterly literary magazine, a party where everyone would be smart and the women would wear outfits that you couldn't figure out how they put on. Like, did they make it at home from scraps of fabric, tying each flowing piece onto some foundation garment? Or did an avant-garde local designer make it at home from scraps of fabric, tying each flowing piece onto some foundation garment? So much draping going on. And someone has had the foresight to strap his oboe case onto the back of his Ducati.

More wine wends its away around the room, deep plum balloons this time. An excerpt of a yet-to-be-staged play is read by live actors, both wearing those long tibia-brushing scarves. But Date Night is on a schedule here, tick tock for the sleeping teen, so goodbye cruel whirls, we have a dinner reso! We throw open the door of the café and face the cold, just as a perfect specimen of wood-fired artisanal pizza is being delivered to a man sitting alone at a table under a people warmer. He looks down at the pizza and then up at me and says, "Leaving already? Sit down and have some pizza with me!"

"Oh," I say, glancing at my husband.

It's the man who directed *The Godfather*.

"We have to run!" I say.

Apocalypse Now.

"We're going to dinner," my husband explains.

The Conversation.

"Really?" He can't believe it. "Here's dinner. Come on, sit down!" he commands.

I look behind me, a classic, just to make sure he's not talking to somebody else.

Oh, what a welcoming bear he is, pawing his warm pizzetta, but we can't even look him in the eye. We skitter down the street, the words on our clouds of breath reading Thank You and Have A Good Night as we head to the homey Italian place with the goofy disco waiters. The place is almost empty and the food's gone downhill, but we try extra hard to be nice to each other, to be extra entertaining, all on our own.

A Visit to Lenscrafters

THERE WAS A PERIOD AROUND 1990 WHEN Daryl Hannah was often seen wearing a pair of large, black-framed glasses. I liked how she looked in them, her delicate face with those giant frames sitting on it. I didn't get the sense that she was only trying to look smart, it also seemed like she was disguising herself a bit or trying on another public face. Usually the job of sunglasses, but more interesting.

Maybe one of the reasons her look appealed to me is because I refused to wear sunglasses at the time. Whenever I put on a pair I immediately felt embarrassed. Oh, look how cool I am, a young person in sunglasses! As stupid as it sounds, I wish more young people would try this out for even a week or so. You don't need a semester at sea to learn about how other people live. Just try walking around without sunglasses for a bit. I think about this every morning as I check out my bold crow's-feet and marvel at how I could have retarded their growth had I been less self-conscious, less of an idiot, and most of all, less of a squinter. Who goes to the beach and the park and the mountains and drives a car all over California for over a decade without sunglasses? Me. I did. But a pair of prescription eyeglasses I didn't even need? That sounded like a great idea.

One morning I popped by the ol' Lenscrafters and told them I needed reading glasses. They tested my eyesight. It was 20/20. I repeated my request. I told them what I really needed were some glasses, please, for reading, for when I had a lot of reading for school and my eyes were getting tired. The guy looked at me for that extra second, his lips parted, pre-sigh. Fine, he said. I selected a pair of heavy black frames, not unlike Daryl Hannah's, made by Esprit.

Esprit was a company I had supported through high school by wearing their colorful logo splashed across crewneck sweatshirts and paired with their striped or polka-dotted pants. I felt loyal to the brand, and feeling loyal to a brand of glasses I didn't need almost convinced me that I possibly needed them, because maybe they needed me. The guy had them put some slightly magnified lenses in them and rang me up. I had just paid a hundred dollars for glasses I didn't need, with lenses you could buy at the drugstore, when I made five dollars an hour at my part-time job. A few hours later they were ready, and I returned and walked proudly out onto the sidewalk with my reading glasses on my face.

I wore the glasses around for a couple of weeks, whenever I remembered to put them on, which wasn't very often because I didn't need them to see so I kept forgetting about them. One afternoon I was walking across campus and a woman stopped me and said, I like your glasses. Those are cool glasses. She was from *Seventeen* magazine and they were doing a fashion feature on my school. She asked if they could photograph me in front of the bike racks. I remember I was wearing cut-off olive green army surplus shorts, a 1970s mustard-yellow men's dress shirt with the collar buttoned to the top, white kneesocks, and bulbous black Doc Martens Mary Janes. And my glasses. Flawless.

We walked over to the bike rack, where I posed with my little red vinyl book bag on top of someone else's bike. Then she asked me to give her a quote about why I rode my bike to school. I told her I didn't ride my bike to school, I either took the bus or drove. She asked me if I ever had ridden my bike to school and I said, a couple times. Then she asked me to give her a quote, but phrase it in the present tense as if I had just ridden my bike to school, presumably the bike that I was posing in front of. I was partially outraged. This was exactly the kind of thing I'd been learning about in my Intro to Media Studies class! See, the media sometimes manipulate how they want the story to be read.

"But if I said that, that would be a lie, wouldn't it?" I volleyed in an attempt to display my critical thinking skills to the writer of a campus fashion piece for a magazine for teenage girls.

"Listen, do you want to be in the magazine or not?"

"Actually," I replied as the sun glinted off the silver buckles on my shoes, "I guess I ride my bike here enough to feel okay about saying I do."

Wasn't really true. Felt like a lie.

"And do you do it for the environment?" she baited.

That was going too far. "No," I said. "I do it for exercise because I think going to the gym is lame." As long as I was lying, I might as well make it sound like something I would say.

When the magazine came out, there I was smiling in my cool outfit with my big glasses, quoted as saying I ride my bike to campus because I care about the environment and because it's great exercise!

When I was packing to move recently, I found a box with the old Esprit glasses in them. My eyesight is worse now, so I popped them on and guess what? They're perfect for reading. And at this point, they're practically vintage.

Ding Dong

WHEN WE MOVED INTO OUR HOUSE IN BERKELEY, a construction worker friend recommended we change our electric clothes dryer over to a gas one. The dryer was only about a year old, but it would be better for our energy bill if we switched it out. He hauled the old dryer into the backyard where it sat for a few months until I was adequately inspired to put it on Craigslist. A few hours after I got the ad up, a guy emailed me. I ran downstairs, wiped it off, and he arrived in a pickup truck later that afternoon. I remember him being an adorable, rural type. About fifty, clean-shaven with a trucker cap and a flannel shirt. He said his daughter was going to UC Berkeley and he was out here from Montana helping her get her new place together.

"What a nice dad!" I gushed. "You came all the way here and you're buying a dryer for your daughter! Wow, she is really lucky!"

He seemed a little surprised by my effusiveness, which often comes whooshing out of me like a seismic wave. Luckily, I've gotten better at reading social cues and have learned how to stuff it back in.

"Well, this dryer is literally only a year old and it's a great deal," I continued.

"And why are you getting rid of it?"

"We switched to a gas one."

"Well, it seems perfect. It's in great shape."

"Yep, only a year old," I said.

"Okay, well that all sounds great."

And then came the fatal move. Reflexively, while he's talking, he opens the dryer door. Then he slams it shut.

"What?" I asked. "Is there a dead rat in there?"

I always think there's going to be a dead rat somewhere. About 40 percent of the time I open any cabinet, closet, or drawer, I think I'm going to see a dead rat. Only ever happened once.

I opened the door and looked in. Sitting there in my dryer was a foot-long, sparkly purple dildo. I had never seen it before.

"Oh my god!" I yelled. "I have NO idea how that got in there. I have never seen that before in my life!"

Bless this man's heart, this upstanding Montana dad who was so put off by me and my dildo dryer that he said his terse thank-you and walked down my driveway, got back in his truck, and drove away.

I called my husband Eli immediately and told him the story.

"Oh no!" he said. "I forgot about that thing!"

"It's yours?"

"Remember when I had that band called Sparklecock?"

I remembered. It was before I met him.

"Well, one time when Nao came to record with me, she brought that as a present. A sparkly cock. She used to work at Good Vibrations."

What was it doing in the dryer?

"I don't know! I think maybe someone I didn't know very well was coming over and I didn't want them to see it, so I threw it in there and forgot about it."

Of course. That's what happens in many of our lives. We want so badly to please the straight-shooting dad, but we are always forgetting about the dong in our dryers.

Baby

Safely on the bed
On his back like they teach us
Monitor crackles

Wine with my mother
What a nap he is having
Never naps for this long

Sprint to the bedroom
My god where is he

A cry muffled by carpet
Never on my knees faster
Up with the flowered bedskirt

How long was he here
How long has it been

Elvis

MY CHEEKBURN FROM THE CREAM-COLORED carpeting was ever-reddening when I first heard your voice coming through to me. Out of my white clock radio you sang about the radio. I got up off my bedroom floor and grabbed the receiver from the beige wall-mounted hall phone. The cord barely stretched into my room, but I shut the door on it, and leaned back. Before dialing, I flipped an invisible switch, the one I hoped would turn a twelve-year-old's voice into a seventeen-year-old's voice. "Who did you just play?" I asked the deejay. "That song 'Radio' I think it's called where the words go *Radio Radio*? Who is that again?" He told me your name was Elvis and it blew me away that there could be another guy who played the guitar and sang in this world named Elvis. I wrote it down on a piece of paper and kept it on my desk. Like I'd forget. Who were you, Other Elvis? Where were you from? How old were you? What kind of shoes did you wear? What kind of thing did you have going on with your hair?

When I came home from school I would turn on the radio and if they hadn't played you after two songs, I would call up and request you. Sometimes they'd play you, but sometimes it was reggae time. In the spring I got to take my virgin BART ride to Berkeley with my friend. BART was a new commuter train. Passing through Fremont, Milpitas, San Leandro, and Oakland, it had modern carpeting and upholstered seats like everything in the future would.

At the record store on Telegraph Avenue I found you and your *This Year's Model*. Look at those glasses! How many questions those glasses posed to my still-growing brain. Maybe those glasses meant you weren't going out on a lot of dates. Maybe those glasses meant you weren't into slutty groupie girls and slutty groupie girls wouldn't like you anyway because they couldn't get past your glasses. Maybe with those glasses you would like a girl like me when I got older. I would make out with you now, as an eighth-grader, but I think those glasses meant you weren't the kind of adult man who would make out with an eighth-grader, but maybe you would wait for me. You could date until then, I was fine with that, because you would probably pick someone nice. But not as nice as me! I promise. I went home to meat loaf and potatoes and milk, and for years I thought I had a chance, a real chance, to be your girlfriend someday. Because of your glasses.

Moe!

EIGHT MONTHS PREGNANT AND I'M FEELING PRETTY COCKY. I've gained about sixty pounds, my hair is newly thick and full, and my boobs have finally crossed into B-cup territory. What better way to celebrate the fact that your pregnancy has gone full term than going to the performance of a fifty-piece orchestra in an Oakland warehouse that culminates with the bandleader, a guy who spells his name with an exclamation point at the end, destroying a piano with a sledgehammer.

Check out the pregnant lady. She looks so funny! Look how her arms hang long like Joey Ramone's, but her stomach is all beachball-like and huge!

Any woman who has been pregnant, if she has any self-awareness at all, will admit to feeling kind of dumb. Not dumb like "pregnancy brain" or whatever those blogs call it, but dumb like a fool. I mean, there you are with your big dumb belly and you're like, "I'm making a baby in here. I'm doing the most important job in the world: growing a human! Something very special is happening in my body and we can all see it."

I was enjoying being stared at. As a woman with medium brown hair, no tattoos, and only a light mustache, I tend to be one of the least interesting of my friends to look at. What began as ambivalence about my appearance has developed into a very conscious personal philosophy. *Don't look at me. There's not too much going on over here.* Except now it was very obvious something was going on with me. And especially in this room of people who were mostly in their twenties. They were at least a hundred years away from having a kid.

In this moment of feeling temporarily powerful, Moe! starts destroying the piano and everyone is cheering. I've actually seen this piece before so I'm standing near the back, soaking up any praise I can, and suddenly a piece of piano shrapnel comes flying through the air and smacks me square in the face. My nose starts bleeding and a metal fragment has cut my lip, so then my lip swells and starts bleeding. And just like when I was ten and got hit in the face with a flying butcher knife, resulting in a veil of blood covering my face and my hands and shirt as I was rushed to the emergency room, I do not want to wipe the blood off for some reason. I want to stand there with the warm ooze streaming down my face for as long as I can. Something about it feels good, feels right. I am a pregnant nightlife columnist with a fat lip and blood streaming down my face and onto my maternity clothes, and I want to feel this way forever.

Public Service Announcement

DON'T HAVE SEX TO A PORTISHEAD RECORD.

There are people who walk among us who will put on a certain kind of record because it is sexy to them. They want to have sex with you to that record. It's their sex record. This person might even have a loosely choreographed sex routine that goes along with the tracks as the record progresses. They have things in mind. Certain songs are good for certain acts. The record makes them feel sexy and they want it to make you feel sexy, too. Feeling sexy together to a Portishead record is something they would like to do. Where were they the first time they heard the Portishead record? Were they in a café or a restaurant and suddenly overcome with a really sexy feeling? Did they go and buy the record thinking, "I can't wait for the next person I want to have sex with to come into my life so we can have sex to this record." What record did it replace? What was the sex record before the Portishead record? How many sex records are there? What sex record is next?

Demo

I HAD A BAND FOR A LITTLE WHILE called The Beth Lisick Ordeal. The short description is that I would tell stories or rant about things while my musician friends played their instruments really well. One night we had a show at the Café du Nord in San Francisco and we heard that Eric Drew Feldman was coming to see us. Eric was famous for being in Captain Beefheart's Magic Band, and had played and recorded with Pere Ubu, Frank Black, and PJ Harvey. All the guys in my band were complete music nerds, and we were flattered that someone with such a weirdo pedigree would be interested in us.

After the show, as we sat at the bar having drinks, Eric told us he'd like us to go into the studio with him and make a demo of our new songs. The idea was that he would produce it for free and if it lead to a record deal he would get a cut off the back end. This seemed ideal since I didn't think the band was very marketable. We were a spoken-word band that featured occasional trombone solos. If Eric could make us seem cool, he deserved all the money he could get.

He booked time at one of the city's oldest and most respected recording studios, located in the Tenderloin. As we loaded our gear in through the doors, we looked at all the photos of the bands who had recorded there: Dead Kennedys, Tupac, George Clinton, Willie Nelson, Jefferson Airplane. Every time I looked at a shiny flat surface, I imagined Grace Slick doing a fat line of coke.

It wasn't lost on us for a second that Eric had been everywhere, knew everyone, and was volunteering his time to work with us. On the first day, he brought me in to meet the owner of the studio, who was supposed to be a big deal, and all of a sudden we were in his office talking about money. Well, the owner talked about money from the other side of his small wooden desk.

"Listen," he said, leaning forward on his elbows. He looked like a hundred other middle-aged white men in the arts to me. Receding hairline, long in the back with a whisper of a curl on hunched shoulders. Perfectly upstanding rock dude with a mortgage. "We have to strike some kind of deal here," he said.

Because he was giving us the use of his expensive studio free of charge, he wanted some kind of percentage on the back end of any deal we got. I was caught off guard. I thought the studio was included in Eric's deal. We had agreed to pay the engineer his day rate and now we had to promise money to this guy, too?

I talked it over with the band. We were pretty good about whipping ourselves into a self-righteous frenzy over the slightest thing back then. We decided that we didn't want to OWE anybody anything, man! I had been working office jobs for the past few years, saving money so I could eventually quit and spend more time writing. I had some money. How much could a few days at a recording studio cost?

I walked into his office the next day with my checkbook in hand and coolly asked him for the amount. When he said it, I tried not to flinch. It was almost everything I had. But there was no turning back. My pride was on the line. I wrote the check and emptied my savings. Demo never went anywhere. The band broke up. Five thousand dollars, I've never been able to save that much since.

Retirement Fund

WHEN I DID MY TAXES ABOUT TEN YEARS AGO, I owed eleven hundred bucks to the IRS. An accountant told me that what I could do instead was put that money into something called a SEP-IRA, a retirement fund for self-employed people.

I went down to Charles Schwab because that's where the guy told me to go. Instead of doing any research on my own, I just walked in the door with my checkbook and said, "Hey, I need to open some kind of account thing called a SEP-IRA."

While some people's M.O. in life is to act like they know what's going on, I am the opposite. I tend to act like I don't know what's going on. Most of the time, I really don't, but sometimes it just seems easier. Instead of Fake It Til You Make It, I'm more like I'm Kind of Making It, I Think, But It Feels Like I Must Be Faking It Because Making It Has Got To Feel Different Than This, So What Is Life?

It was easy to locate someone who would take my check. Then there was some other step I was supposed to take. Diversifying the funds? Making some kind of choice? "Putting" it somewhere, like on your computer when you can create a file folder inside another file folder? All I remember is the guy said that there was another step I needed to do and it involved options, but I couldn't choose an option, so he said that I could call and do it later by phone. That's the option I always take. The one that allows me to "deal with it later."

When I walked out the door, my memory of the whole experience was essentially wiped clean. Statements would arrive;

quarterly, I imagine, and I would get a vague tinge of something. The way I suspect an animal in a petting zoo remembers a kid trying to feed it a dime. Something happened here, but what? A chalk outline of a memory. But honestly, why bother thinking about it? It was the money I was supposed to let sit there and accumulate. After I did the thing.

One day while reading Suze Orman for the book I was writing about the self-help industry, I decided to open up the statements. They must be earning a little interest, and Suze convinced me to stop being so clueless about my personal finances. I went to the drawer and opened up the most recent one. My account had less than four hundred dollars in it. I think it's because I didn't do the thing.

Uncherried

TODAY WAS THE DAY I BOUGHT MY FIRST CAR with money I saved from answering telephones in a professional manner. If anything can prepare you for a life of keeping it together, this has got to be it. Your own car? Come on. And it's a fucking bitchin' car. 1966 Ford Falcon. Original chrome rims. Not a V-8, not a slant six, but some other thing, a straight six. I practice saying it with two different inflections so it will sound natural when someone asks me what's under the hood. It's a straight six, a straight six. Brand new paint. Midnight blue. Perfect interior. Royal blue leather. Flawless white headliner and sun visors.

I found the car on a website, which is a new invention that allows the computer at my office to connect to other cyberworlds via my modem. The Uniform Resource Locator (or URL as they are called) can be found at http://www.craigslist.org (which is all one word, no spaces) but people refer to it as "Craig's List." A local computer nerd named Craig started it so you can sell your sofa or find a roommate more easily, but only if you live in San Francisco.

When the gangster kid drives it into the abandoned lot in Hunters Point where we've agreed to meet, it is so beautiful that I well up. He says he needs to sell it in a hurry and will take fifteen hundred. It had never occurred to me to name my previous cars, the Honda Accord I shared with my brother or the Toyota pickup I inherited from my dad, but as I hand over my bills and my ass sinks into the soft palm of the Falcon's perfect seats, I start thinking of one. Grover, like the Sesame Street character, because of it color, or maybe another presidential name like Rutherford or Chester or Ulysses S.

The minute I roll into Oakland boys are pulling up next to me at stoplights and laying it on me, giving me the ultimate: *You wanna sell it? You wanna sell it?*

I just smile and yell, "No! I just bought it!"

So tonight's my turn to bring beer to band practice, and nowadays we do two sixers. That's three beers each for a two-hour rehearsal, which we've found to be the perfect amount of buzz-to-competence ratio. And those guys are going to freak out over my car, so of course we're all going to have to go over to the Albatross later for tequila.

I pull into the lot next to the liquor store, put the car in park, and lock the door. Hey, the kid even had it outfitted with an alarm. Even though I'm only walking twenty yards away, I try it out for fun. *Beep beep!*

I'm two strides down the lot when I get the sense that there's a ghost on my trail. It's nearly silent under the stars. A low creak makes me turn my head just in time to see my brand new car piloting itself through the parking lot, rolling backwards across the asphalt, a slow-burn poem as it goes with the flow down the embankment until it comes to a rest with a chunky crunch against a grocery cart stable. For the very first time, that car alarm in the night, the one that won't ever go off, is mine.

Wedged up against the metal like that, the driver's side door won't open. I slip in the passenger side, fire it up, and keep flooring the gas, revving, until we're violently wrenched free with a sphincter-tightening *screeeeeeeeeeech.*

I bag the beer mission and head to rehearsal. A tunnel of lights shoots across the gravel as I cripple it into the lot of the warehouse, suspension tweaked, driver's side punched in, alarm still honking.

Hey, guys. Come check out my brand-new ride. I just bought it today.

Office Holiday Party

THE BIG CHRISTMAS PARTY WAS COMING UP. I had been working at the Fog City Diner for a few months, but I hadn't met many of the other people who worked there because of my baker's hours. I came in at 4 a.m., and by the time I left the lunch service was in full swing and everyone was slammed. The party was going to be held at Tosca, a legendary San Francisco bar I'd heard about but never been to. That, combined with the fact that I had the next day off, was enough to make me build this party up like it was going to be the most momentous occasion of my life. And maybe it was. I was twenty-two. I was new to the city. I worked at a restaurant that was recently featured on an American Express commercial and I was going to a bar where Sean Penn hung out. Finally, it was on. Things were happening in my adult life.

I wore an ivory-colored cocktail dress from the '60s that had spaghetti straps, hit just above the knee, and had a single row of small white barbell-shaped beads below the bustline. Usually I chose more clownlike, Phyllis Diller getups, but I wanted my first impression to be classy and sophisticated. Like the dress could play tricks on everyone.

I saw an empty stool at the bar, right near the door, and immediately sat down. This would work for a while, watching the party in the mirror's reflection, scanning the crowd of glamorous Food People working in a Food Town. I'd catch part of my own image, my hand holding the champagne flute or my lips in that shade the lady at the MAC counter had told me looked good, and I'd create a story about where I fit in. I knew I wasn't that much of an outsider, I had worked in restaurants before, but Santa Cruz seemed like a different world. For instance, my old chef had once roller-skated around the dining room wearing only an apron. I checked my hair again and waited to move until I saw Robert, the chef who'd hired me. He brought me around to meet the owners and the bartenders and the wait staff. There were a few line cooks I recognized. We overlapped a little at work, but were always too busy to talk.

When I ran into Jennifer, the head baker who worked for all the restaurants owned by this same restaurant group, I was still a little nervous. Everybody called Jennifer a saint because she put hundreds of miles on her car every week traveling to their restaurants in Sonoma, Napa, and San Francisco, coming up with new recipes and doing all the ordering for the bakeshops. Whenever she'd stop in at Fog City, she would give me a hand with my work and show me new tricks. When I excused myself to go to the bathroom, she told me to come back and find her. I remember feeling relieved to have been given a post-toilet assignment. When I returned we continued our talk and she told me that a lot of the kitchen staff hadn't gone to culinary school either, but had learned like I did, working in a series of kitchens over the years. I saw a real career opening up for me. You put in your years and then you get to develop recipes and create menus. We might have been talking about the vagaries of bread-proofing on foggy days, a hot topic in San Francisco, when one of the line cooks sitting in a booth waved me over from across the room. I made my way to her table, noticing a few heads turning.

"Lisick," she said. "We were just sitting here debating whether we should tell you or not. Douglas thinks we should, but I was all for not saying anything."

"What? Tell me what?"

This story has taken on a new cast with time because when I tell you now that my dress was tucked into my nylons, exposing my entire flank to the room, and it had been that way since I'd exited the bathroom roughly fifteen minutes before, what mortifies me most is that I was wearing suntan-colored nylons and thought they looked sophisticated.

Carolyn the line cook reached over, yanked my dress out of my waistband and smoothed it down, ending the gesture with a slap on my ass. I turned in horror to see everyone looking over and laughing, like a scene in a student film where the student is trying be Felliniesque. If I had been working there longer, or was older, or knew more people, it probably wouldn't have been as bad; Lord knows I have done this at least a few times since. But when I imagine the young me, trying to be sophisticated, sashaying around the room like I thought I was fucking Audrey Hepburn with a killer crème brûlée technique, it's devastating.

The next morning I woke up in a shame pit. I heard my boyfriend recounting the story to our roommate, who got out of the shower, came into my room, and laughed in my face about it while wearing a towel. Then the two of them left for work, keeping the radio tuned to the Alex Bennett morning show. Alex Bennett was on the alternative rock station and even though he had a lot of smart comedians as guests, Alex himself was bitter and mean. It was a call-in show, and as I lay in bed listening, I decided to call in for the first time. I don't know why I thought calling big bad dad Alex Bennett to confess my sins would make me feel better.

"I went to my office Christmas party last night," I said, knowing that the set-up was already a winner. They actually responded with a kind of Oh boy. Here we go attitude that gave me the momentum I needed. "And I accidentally tucked my dress into my nylons and walked around like that for a pretty long time before anyone told me."

In response to that, Alex and his comedian guest and the studio audience laughed a lot. And not in the "I've been there, sister!" way that would have been more comforting.

"Oh, lady," Alex said. "I know your type! Probably got drunk and tried to hit on your boss, too. You might as well just quit your job because everyone there thinks you're a whore anyway."

I panicked and hung up. It was like penance with no absolution.

When I went to work the next day, my boss told me they were listening to the show in the kitchen and heard me. They never listened to Alex Bennett! They usually had ranchero music on.

"Ugh, that was so terrible!" I said. "I was so embarrassed, and then calling the show just made me feel worse about it."

He looked at me like I was an idiot. "Then why did you do it?"

I tried to ask my brain what kind of answer would go here. Why do you call a radio station with thousands of listeners to tell them something that made you feel horrible?

"I don't know," I said.

He laughed. "Well, let me know when you figure it out."

Hooker

MY ALARM WOULD GO OFF AT THREE-THIRTY A.M. and I had to be at work on the other side of town by four. This meant that I would roll out of bed, put on my checked pants and white coat, brush my teeth and hair, walk out into the darkness, get in my truck and take Valencia to Market to Franklin to Broadway to the Embarcadero and park six blocks away from the restaurant in a rare forever spot, one I could stay in for my whole shift. Then I would jog down the middle of Battery Street because that seemed like the safest thing to do at that hour. I'd unlock the door, get the coffee going, and drink just about the whole pot before anyone else even got to work. During these commutes I saw:

> dark shapes hovering in bushes
> trucks blowing through red lights
> cars weaving across lanes
> raccoons staring me down
> a wild dog in a dead sprint
> dead dogs and smashed cats
> flocks of seagulls
> cruise ships coming in
> tugboats going out
> businessmen in suits on empty streets waiting for signals to
>   change
> women hunched over sewing machines bathed in yellow
>   light
> shadows moving around inside closed bars

an apartment building, dark except for blue TV glow
    flickering from two separate apartments, as if they
    were watching the same channel
police checking me out as I checked them out

One morning as I drove in the darkness a truck in front of me slammed on its brakes. I watched as the driver's side door opened and a woman was thrown out, sent tumbling into the middle of the street. I didn't stop to check on her. I didn't roll down my window and ask if she was okay. I didn't call anyone. I didn't do anything. I waited for her to get up and limp away and then I went to work.

A Powerful Evening of
Spoken-Word Performance

THE SHOW WAS AT A DUSTY OLD THEATER downtown that some-one was trying to revitalize. That's always a great idea, but what's not always a great idea is programming an evening with a line-up of spoken-word poets. I'm sorry, Def Poetry Jam. I'm sorry, poetry slammers. It's not you, it's me. Well, sometimes it's you, too.

When I think about myself standing on a stage reciting short memorized stories and poems, rapid-fire, twitching, teeming with angst, I feel covered in a mild film of self-loathing. What drew me to it, I think, is that it was the first type of performing I had ever seen that I understood how to make happen myself: Just write something short, commit it to memory, and then go onstage and try to make the audience feel something. I had spent all of my college years being silent in the back, wondering how people got to be so bold, writing and speaking with such authority when we were all so young. It took me years after getting out of a classroom to start to find a voice. And apparently that voice could be very loud and declarative! Hopefully when I'm an old lady I'll be able to find it brave or beautiful, but now it seems similar to the time I shaved my head and threw all my clothes in a bathtub full of black Rit dye. Absolutely necessary in the moment, but kind of stinky and sloppy.

This story comes from when I was in the thick of it. Back when I had only been performing for about a year and was nervous to be doing a show in a real theater, instead of the usual smoky bars. During an intermission, I went to the restroom. It didn't seem like I was in there for very long, but from inside the stall, I heard the emcee starting up the show again.

I can hear that she's doing an intro and suddenly I realize it's my intro. I jump off the toilet, pull my pants up, and run down the center aisle of the theater, checking to make sure I don't have toilet paper streaming from my shoe. Unable to see how to get onto the stage, I hoist myself up and shoulder-roll onto it. That felt pretty cool. I also decided that instead of pretending that I'd planned this, I should acknowledge what had just happened.

"Hey, everybody." I say as I brush my hands on my pants. "Sorry about that. I was literally sitting on the toilet when I heard my name being called."

There are a few laughs, which relax me, and I begin my set. Things about car wrecks and fake 12-step groups and gated communities. Keep in mind that I am naturally a bit spastic of body. If I am making the leap into being unselfconscious, into genuinely committing to express myself, my body will do all sorts of things I'm not in control of. This is probably why professional performers take classes or workshops. As I hurtle forth into my next poem, limbs loose and flailing, I notice something. A rustling sound. Someone brownbagging a beer perhaps? Except it sounds closer than even the front row. I continue full speed ahead, but I keep hearing the rustle. And then it dawns on me: the sound is coming from inside my pants.

You know how a toilet seat cover sticks to your ass sometimes? Probably because your ass is sweaty, but anyway, in my rush to get off the toilet and onto the stage, I pulled up my underwear and pants in one fell swoop with the toilet seat cover attached to my ass. With a spotlight trained on my every action, I attempt to shove this toilet seat cover below the waistband of my pants until it morphs into a noticeable tube on my lower back.

I wish I had been brave enough to just rip it out, hold it up like Yorick's skull and tell everyone what had happened. I think the only thing not embarrassing about this story is that it proves I can sometimes be concerned about sanitary issues. Jesus. Maybe this is my way of bragging that I sometimes use toilet seat covers.

Pig

SINI AND I WOKE UP IN THE TOUR VAN, which was parked on the back lawn of some communal living space in Atlanta. All the doors were thrown open because it was August and already so sticky, even before the sun came blasting in on us. I thought about the woman at that bar crushing the beer cans between her boobs when we heard a noise. A grunt. We looked outside and saw an enormous pig wandering into the house where everybody else was sleeping. Inside the house, our friend skittered out from a bedroom with duct tape all over her wrists and ankles. It was probably smart to have slept in the van. How had we ended up parked on that back lawn anyway? Sini thought I drove. I thought she did.

Mystery Sniff

IT'S THE THIRD OR FOURTH STOP WE'VE MADE after our show here in New Orleans, the place after the place where the Etch-a-Sketch played a role in our bar brawl. The black-and-white hexagonal tiles are grimy and the grout is caked black. I'm staring down at my pink flip-flops, my anklebones doing a Butoh-wobble as I hover and pee, when a credit card is passed underneath the stall. Atop it is a tiny sprinkling of white powder. This is drugs. This is something I don't do.

Recently, a close friend was telling me about a friend of hers whose overseas volunteer job had gotten gummed up because she'd had to undergo a psychiatric evaluation, which labeled her as manic. This woman was forty-six years old and had never been diagnosed as having any kind of behavioral disorder. As we ate our burrata or whatever it was, some soft cheese at a semi-Italian place, we expressed our mutual disbelief.

"Oh my god," I said. "I'm sure if I went through that, they would say I was manic, too."

My friend paused for a beat and then looked at me like I was smoldering, like I was just about extinguished, and said in the lame sarcastic cadence of a TV character thirty years her junior, *Well, yeah!* Like the same annoying way people say *Just sayin'!* I hadn't expected her to agree with such alacrity.

I get excited sometimes. I believe in the power of an affectionate greeting for one whom you have not seen in a while. And when I get on a roll, a tequila and chitchat roll, I am sometimes possessed by a strange surge of energy that makes me incapable of disengaging until the night is definitely, for sure, as announced by everyone else, over. But I honestly don't think I'm manic. For instance, I don't not sleep. I have only stayed up all night a handful of times in my life. Yes, there was this one time when I was laying in bed trying to conk out and my brain couldn't stop repeating *BILL HEEHAN, BILL HEEHAN, BILL HEEHAN*, a pseudonym a friend had made up to write record reviews in the '90s. And one time, after a long flight to Nairobi, I heard the voice of my British hostess echoing the phrase *BIBS AND BOBS* approximately one thousand times as I lay on a single futon in the dark, but on the whole I do not conduct my daily life under the sway of any unusual brain chemistry surges. I generally feel centered, if slightly pumped. I don't need drugs. The thought of me on drugs scares me.

So there I stood in the grimy bathroom stall, looking at the credit card attached to some anonymous hand, and I grabbed it and I snorted it, up my right nostril, the larger opening of my deviated septum. Then I danced and ate beignets, went to sleep on a hardwood floor and woke up covered with red welts. Those lasted until Georgia.

Yokohama Threeway

WHICH MOVIE STAR DO YOU LOOK LIKE? That's a game that Japanese people used to like to play with white people in the early '90s. I don't know if they play it anymore now that white people and movie stars are easier to view on your computer than ever before, but the best one I ever got: Babala Stleisandu.

I was hoping the old man at the ramen house meant the *What's Up Doc?* Babala Stleisandu as opposed to the *Prince of Tides* Babala Stleisandu, but everyone covered their mouths and made high-pitched noises of light embarrassment. One lady even tried to make me feel better by saying it was only because of my nose. That was all. Just a little like Barbra in the nose.

Now, Jodie Foster. She was who my friend got all the time. And something about the fact that I was in Japan made me not care about being the Yentl to her Clarice Starling. Really, most of that month in Yokohama was spent in a similar state of not caring much about whatever was happening, in alternately glorious and insidious ways. For instance, I was eating stinky tofu and wearing mismatched socks a lot, things I never did back home. Plus lying around naked in close proximity to my naked friend and her naked man friend.

Such a dirty bird, he was. Where did he get off anyway? Wait, I know this one. Right on my face, apparently. In my eye.

Which leads me to a tiny Q&A.

Q: What do you call a middle-aged British man who

has been living in Japan for fifteen years and has yet to
learn to speak the language?
A: A pervert.

Q: What is wrong with being a pervert?
A: Nothing.

Q: Why are you being a jerk then?
A: Sometimes it just seems like there are a lot of dudes
who are into plaid skirts and coming on your face.

Q: So pedestrian versions of "nonconformity" make you
agitated?
A: I think it's Burning Man syndrome. Sometimes I
lash out.

That first night at dinner he was okay. Said I reminded him
of a cat, which I think was supposed to be a compliment, but that
is just judging from Halloween costumes that grown women wear.
But in the middle of my inaugural threeway, on a futon in a room
with rice paper doors and a tatami mat, it hit me. I was one of two
California girls, fresh out of college, currently doing it with a weird
older guy. In Japan, even, the mysterious land of sexual pleasure.
Bang a gong.

Straddling one or the other, I thought, Huh, so when the
last of bit of my flesh chars in the crematorium, I will have been
a woman who helped a mediocre man live out a classic scenario
from Penthouse Forum.

This guy had a method for drying off after a shower that he
enjoyed sharing with new friends. Before you reach for the towel,
sort of squeegee yourself with the palm of your hand first. Squeegee down the length of one arm, shake off the water, and then the
other, shake off the water, then down one leg, shake off the water,
and then the other. Shake off the water. The point is to save your

towel from getting soaked. This actually ended up proving useful in later years while living in damp, cave-like apartments where there was no natural light and a thin coating of mold crept rapidly over my shoe leather.

I still think of him just after turning off the shower, right before I reach for the towel. I bet somewhere out there, someone has named their cat Barbra Streisand.

It Girl

IT WASN'T DUSTY AND IT WASN'T STEVIE AND it wasn't Davie and it wasn't Johnny and it wasn't Bobbie and it wasn't Mickey and it wasn't Scotty and it wasn't Matty and it wasn't Jerry and it wasn't Charlie, but it was the name Ron used to always call me. A name for a boy, but worked for a girl.

I'd never heard of her, the girl I reminded him of, but some of the old-timers at the bar had. *Classic It Girl*, he'd say, and then point to me and go, *like her*. And the drunks would look me up and down, unimpressed.

In the morning at work we'd all be a bit fragile, with our coffees and egg sandwiches from Tortilla Flats, and there he would be reaching down under his desk. Room temp PBR that he'd pull up can after can throughout the day from a case at his feet. He'd offer you one, offer anybody one, and in the beginning we'd all have one. But then when we'd go to the bar after work he would nurse his drink, barely touching it until it looked like everyone was leaving to go somewhere else. I'd turn around and the entire thing would be gone. Drained. I found out later that he would buy a pint, go across the street to his apartment, down a couple of beers real quick, and then come back.

One night at the Fillmore his girlfriend tried to strangle me. She was a gorgeous blonde with big boobs and a lazy eye. Can you take it? Does it get better than that? And then to have her soft, icy hands wrapped around my throat, squeezingsqueezing in slo-mo while everyone tried to pull her off? It was the first time I'd met her, so she must have heard some horrible things about me. I heard she got sober.

One Saturday morning, I had some sort of weird side job and had to be across the city by 7 a.m. The streets in the Mission were mostly empty, but then I saw a lone figure walking back from the all night Safeway with a case of PBR on his shoulder. Was he up already or still up? I told myself I didn't stop to give him a ride because I didn't want to embarrass him, but I know he wouldn't have cared. He would have been happy to see me. The reason I didn't stop is because I didn't want him in my car. I saw my friend walking down the street and I sank back into my hoodie and cruised right past him.

I spoke at his memorial, held in a dive bar during the day, which was appropriate and depressing, appropriately depressing, whose idea was *that* but I guess where else was it supposed to be. We all had pints, and what I wanted to say to everyone gathered was, *I'm glad.* I'm glad I don't have to get into his rental car that smells like barf and watch his nose and cheeks turning into an Andy Capp comic and pretend to be excited to run into him or try to understand what he's saying and then give him a hug to shut him up. Aren't you all glad you don't have to give him a hug to shut up his drunken mouth anymore? Dead at thirty-eight from his internal organs busting into liquid and coming out his holes. Or maybe that's just how I pictured it.

And what was that name he always called me? I was up late Googling but couldn't put in the right combination of words to riddle it right so I lay in bed scrolling through the names of all the boys I'd ever met until I finally got to Joe. Joey. That's who I reminded him of. Joey Heatherton was her name. She had nice legs and starred in a provocative Serta mattress commercial in the '70s. She's still alive.

My Thing

A TV PRODUCER WANTED TO PITCH A NEW SHOW and she was wondering if I was interested in being the host. This fit in nicely with my career strategy of saying yes to things I would never have pursued on my own. Obviously, other people have a better idea at what you might be good at than you do, right? Doesn't everyone fantasize that something, anything really, will come along in life and suddenly be their "thing"? And everyone will be like, "Wow! You're such a natural! Are you sure you've never done this before?" And you'll be like, "I swear! It's so weird that I've never done this! I'm so good at it, I enjoy it, *and* I'm getting paid more than I've ever made before to do it. Finally, I've found my thing!"

I watched through the window as a feral orange tabby took a shit on my agave plant while the woman on the phone described the show. The idea was that I would be an aging everywoman who was just, you know, exploring new things. I needed to be able to be breezy, accessible, smart, funny, engaging, humble, goofy, confident, and professional while holding a microphone and talking about something I know nothing about. I expertly negotiated on my own behalf to receive a fee of not one but two hundred dollars for an eight-hour day of shooting that started at 6 a.m. And I thought: So maybe this is my thing!

I imagined forays into tango dancing, herbal remedies for water retention, Turkish cooking lessons, and the activity that finds its way into every aspirational show — rock climbing! First at a climbing wall with a young, Argentine instructor who would strap me into the harness while we made vague sexual innuendo, and then later scaling a pretty impressive mountain peak where I would cry real tears of overwhelm at the end, but then do something silly like put my hat on sideways and cross my eyes to let everyone know I was really all right.

The producer thought a good theme for the pilot episode would be an edgy little so-and-so called Beauty Treatments. She asked if I was willing to get Botox on camera, and was I ever. I badmouth that shit all the time, without ever opening my mouth, so as not to offend friends, colleagues, audience members, moms from my kid's school, my hairstylist, or any people who might be on a website called Facebook. I grit my teeth (and then immediately tell myself to stop or my marionette lines will get worse) over my increasingly cartouche-like forehead and permanent pillow scars. How fortuitous to be given the perfect excuse to get my face shot full of poison in the name of quasi telejournalism! Then if I liked the way I looked, I could keep coming up with excuses why I still had it. I actually imagined telling people that somehow, miraculously, those first injections had blocked the nerve impulses in my face in a very permanent way.

"Listen to this," I'd say. "I got Botox once for this lame TV thing I was doing. What? No, I'm not in TV. I just thought it was going to be my thing for a second! Anyway, it paralyzed my forehead permanently and that's why I don't have any wrinkles anymore and won't have them anymore forever until I die. I don't know, I was thinking of suing, but I'm not really into that so I guess I'm stuck with it. Oh, well." Results without the judgment.

I met the producer at a salon in Pacific Heights and the first thing she had me do was undergo a treatment where you sausage yourself into a cotton mesh body stocking, sprawl face down on a table, and let a Brazilian woman assault you with a vibrating hose attached to an enormous whirring machine sitting in the corner. I felt like an industrial carpet in a rental unit being worked over by someone who really needed their deposit back. This violent vacuuming was supposed to break up the cellulite in my ass and thighs, and I was instructed to provide running commentary on what was happening. It wasn't easy to talk with all the noise and the camera guy zooming in on my flanky parts, but I tried to look simultaneously cute and exasperated. Of all the crazy things!

Next up: bikini time. The camera was going to follow me into the anteroom of the spray tan chamber as I got power-bronzed. I thought I had a fairly good idea of what a spray tan entailed. I had seen the home machines on whatever reality show I marathon-watched on the airplane. Okay, it was *Toddlers and Tiaras*. I knew it was different from the beds that you lay in, but somehow I was not prepared.

As soon as they closed me into the chamber, which was really just a filthy glass shower stall with dim lighting and someone's pink Venus razor in the soap dish, I started to get claustrophobic. It already smelled like someone left their feet in a coconut cake for too long, then cranked on the jets. I don't mean to lessen the suffering of anyone who has ever been inside a gas chamber, but the way this works seems gas chamber adjacent. I could have said a steam room, I suppose, but because the substance shooting out of the jets is obviously toxic, I'm going to stick with gas chamber.

Part of the idea is that we were meant to be showcasing businesses around the Bay Area, but there I was ruining it by squirming among the streams of orange mist laugh-yelling, "I feel like I'm getting cancer right now!"

When I got dressed and headed upstairs for the final segment, the "makeover" portion, it was noted that I had pulled the shower cap down too low in the tanning booth, leaving a stark white patch on my forehead. I sat for about a half hour in a salon chair as the makeup artist evened things out. She shaped and darkened my brows, styled my hair into soft waves, and finished me off with glossy lips.

Obviously the point was to make me look better, but it was

humiliating to have to hear from the producer and her brother and the camera guy and the salon owner how much better I now looked. They brought me outside to wrap up the show as passersby stopped to watch what was going on. Well, they would watch for a couple seconds and quickly realize I was nobody talking about nothing and move on. With one of those silver light-bouncing screens aimed at my face, I tried over and over again to good-naturedly sum up my wild day! I was having trouble "nailing it" without making some kind of reference to feeling embarrassed, exhausted, or relieved it was over. In the end, the producer fed me a few lines and I parroted them right back into the camera with a smile on my face; it felt like my cellulite had gotten jostled around and made a beeline right for my brains. This was not my new thing.

Carole-Induced Zit

TARA AND I HAD A COMEDY PERFORMANCE ON Valentine's Day. We needed to come up with something to fill time while we were changing costumes and figured we could make a slide show fairly easily. All we needed was a simple storyline, something that would come across with pictures only, because you should never saddle the soundperson in a small rock club on a weekday night with complicated audio and visual components for your ten-minute set of sketch comedy.

It feels so good to say that with authority because I say almost nothing with authority.

We decided that our characters, Carole and Mitzi, would make some friends on the bus and invite them over to their apartment for pancakes and sex. We didn't even think to show a photo of the bus ride or the pancakes; they are simply implied, part of the backstory. And the sex, of course, just looks like Jazzercise or tumbling where some of the parties (okay, just Carole and Mitzi) are nude. The other people are referred to as their "new friends."

So we're at our friend Michelle's apartment doing the photo shoot, and before we get to the one where Carole and Mitzi are engaging in a platonic 69 — a position where they curl toward each other toe-to-head-head-to-toe for a chat — we do one where Carole is shaving. Shaving her face. (It's a lot more expedient than waxing or threading. I don't know why more women don't just go for it.) We're naked except for our costumes of wigs and glasses, plus my voluminous display of pubic hair, which shouldn't be considered bragging until I reveal to you that it is luxuriant in sheen and softness. I'm looking in the mirror with shaving cream on my face, doing what I think will make a hilarious picture. I put my tongue inside my cheek and push it out hard so that it makes a big ball I can put the razor against. Maybe I saw my dad do this when I was little or maybe I saw it on a TV show or in a cartoon. The bigger the cheek ball I make, the funnier it looks so I keep jabbing my tongue as hard as I can. Tara is cracking up and the picture comes out great. I look like an older man who lives in a studio apartment and eats a lot of canned soup. It's not as funny as the one of Tara as Mitzi wiping herself while she sits on the toilet, but that one's shot from floor level focused directly at her relatively hairless vulva, so it's hard to compete.

The day after the shoot I wake up to an irritation near the corner of my lower lip, about a centimeter off the shore of my mouth. Right where I was making the ball. The next day, there's a hard pebble inside my face, like one of those zits you know is going to hound you for at least a week. A few days later, I wake up to find a pinprick-size tip of white emerging from the utter rock hardness beneath. Next day: same. Next day: same. Next day, I am overcome by the need to move this thing along. I squeeze and squeeze, trying to force the issue, but nothing doing. What if I poke it with a pin? Nothing. What if I tear off the top with my tweezers? Nothing. I go to bed and try to visualize the ideal outcome for all of this. I would be lying if I said I wanted it to simply disappear. I wanted the satisfaction of witnessing its destruction.

Next morning: surprise! Do you remember puberty when perhaps you would play host to a whitehead the size of a pencil eraser? This is what's happening, and it is disgusting and wonderful and a relief. I do what I was born to do and squeeze it until there is a hole in my face.

All of that method acting for a photograph shown to fifty

people at a bar on Valentine's night. This was five years ago and I still have a visible divot in my face. And if you don't know the way aging skin works, lean in because every day it keeps getting a little bigger.

A Short Contest

Welcome to The Dueling Nightstand Drawer Surprises of Two
Men with Ph.Ds!

Because we have been unable to determine a winner for the past
    twenty years
due to severe brain cramping plus a whispered invitation to
    diarrhea
whenever memory decides it's time to play
we have opened up the floor to you:
Let's meet the contestants!

These two finalists make
a rock drummer's Barely Legals or
an energy consultant's poppers and fuzzy handcuffs
look like a couple of Nyquils
nestled in a package of travel Kleenex

The Russian Literature Ph.D. enters the ring with a syringe!
The Astronomy Ph.D. comes out of his corner with a handgun!

We only have time for four questions
and the answers are no
yes, yes, and
it was clear by the way his lips were always wet and he rarely
    blinked.

Now is the time to select a winner or write in the name of your
    own
personal winner here _____.

(Bedside tables that are milk crates covered
in the flag of a country with a decent soccer team
will be disqualified.)

Waterskiing

Dragged in a frog crouch
Didn't let go when falling
First time up on skis

Butt spanked by water
Skittering across the lake
Faces in boat scream

At last I get it
I drop the tow rope and wait
Alone and treading

They come circling back
Teenagers laughing, I'm twelve
Legs shake as I climb

When I'm recovered
Pop a grape Cragmont soda
Look down and notice

Bikini bottom
Bisecting my vagina
For the past half hour

Another surprise
Comes a few minutes later
Tahoe enema

Fuck You, Stephen Elliott

IF YOU ARE EVER INVITED TO PARTICIPATE IN a charity spelling bee, the first question you'll want to ask is: Will Stephen Elliott be there? It's not that the author Stephen Elliott is noted to be a gifted speller of words or known as a legitimate competitor in this arena. As a matter of fact, we don't really know if Stephen Elliott can spell many words at all. Yes, he can write books; critically acclaimed books that have won him fans and supporters across the globe, and we know he is adept at attracting celebrities, politicians, authors and — come to think of it — *dominatrixes* and *sycophants*, both pretty big words themselves, but we do not know anything about his personal aptitude to spell out loud, off the top of his head, in front of an audience. Whatever he was doing on Adderall, it probably didn't include the occasional oral pop quiz, but that's the thing about Stephen. Maybe it did.

I showed up at the gallery where the spelling bee was taking place and my first thought was one I rarely have: *Free alcohol: Let's stay away from that.* I knew that even one small jigger of whatever donated spirit they were pouring was going to knock me off my game. I wanted an edge.

"I can't believe you're taking this seriously," my friend laughed.

"It's not that I want to win, Jan," I said. "It's that I don't want to be humiliated." Okay, I kind of wanted to win.

Ever since a blogger described my voice as an "adenoidal slur" in a write-up of an event that took place at a bar, I've been self-conscious about drinking in public. And ever since the fifth grade when I was knocked out in the final round of the Congress

Springs spelling bee for spelling *demure* d-e-m-u-r, even though Mrs. Hilding clear-as-day pronounced the word as *de-MUR*, leaving out the crucial diphthong so what I spelled was exactly what she had pronounced, and if she had pronounced the fucking word properly, I would have figured out that just like *cure* and *pure*, words I absolutely knew how to spell at age ten, the word *demure* would have the final *e* that causes the *u* to slide into the liquid diphthong sound. I'm sure I had read that word in one of my mom's Sidney Sheldon paperbacks.

Yes, I came into the adult spelling bee that night with a little baggage.

Stephen and I had been talking and as soon as the event started, we sat down next to each other to finish our conversation. Big mistake. I had let him sit to my left, the speller after me. If he had been to my right, I'd have been the one to get the word after he — inevitably? — misspelled it.

A couple rounds in, problems were surfacing. First of all, the acoustics in the art gallery were preposterous. There were high ceilings, wood floors, nearly bare walls, and metal folding chairs. Bless all nonprofessional event organizers, but there has never been decent sound in a room not architecturally designed for performance, where a rented public address system has been hauled in and set up just before the guests arrive. Never.

Secondly, the NPR reporter who was disseminating the words that evening was a little chatty. In my estimation, if you are running a spelling bee, your job is to say the word and only the word. Sure, it's a paid event with booze, and the audience wants a little color commentary from the intelligent public figure, but I found this extremely distracting for doing what I was summoned to do that evening: spell words correctly, without distraction, in hopes of proving that I am amazing.

The fourth round comes up and the speller before me is given the word for the tiny guitar-like instrument popularized by

Don Ho and again, more recently, by a number of indie rock front women from Portland to Brooklyn. The author before me spells this word wrong, though I would have spelled it the same way. Strange. I had always thought it was spelled u-k-u-l-e-l-e, but I supposed it must be the next logical answer, u-k-e-l-e-l-e. I spell it, in a clear voice, one that is only slightly adenoidal by nature but unrelentingly slur-free. And I am cast out. What? Why the laughter? More precisely, why the laughter directed at me? My walk of shame commences as I am dismissed and the word is passed on to Elliott.

I piece it together. Apparently, the person before me had spelled it u-k-e-l-e-l-e and I had misheard it as u-k-u-l-e-l-e and proceeded to spell it incorrectly in the exact same way the person before me had! And when it was Stephen's turn? Well, it should have been obvious for him but I swear I could hear hesitation in his voice, like he wasn't really sure he was getting it right even after all that. But he did. So I had a drink. I tried to forget about it. My friend reminds me this is just a dumb fundraiser after all.

Two days later an article comes out in the paper. The headline reads, "Here, Have a Drink. Now Spell Ukulele."

In the article, a quote from Stephen Elliott:

"I said I was going to beat Tobias Wolff so bad that he would forget his last novel," Elliott said. "That didn't work out, but Beth Lisick misspelled [ukulele] the exact same way as the person before her, which I feel means I beat her in some weird way, because that's the worst possible way to lose a spelling bee. So I look at that as a victory. Definitely. I beat Beth Lisick."

The Panda Ambulance

I GOT AN EMAIL FROM A LADY I'D never met wondering if I would be interested in moderating a book club for a group of six fifth-grade girls and their mothers. She suggested each family would pay forty dollars a session, so that would be $240 a month to find and read a book, come up with discussion questions, and meet with everyone. It sounded fun, and I have done much stranger things for much less money, so I gave her a call.

Oh, wait. First I Googled her and read the article about the Japanese-inspired eco-redesign of her four-story San Francisco Edwardian home, scrolled through the accompanying photos of her master bedroom overlooking the Presidio National Park where the skylights were designed with custom German glass embedded with cells that act as solar-powered magnets, and checked out the modern art piece in the living room, a 3-D mural of twenty inflatable see-through plastic pillows. Then I got her husband's name from the article and Googled him. And then Google image searched him. Then I gave her a call.

Janet and I had an instant rapport that I attributed to both of us feeling very proud of the class divide we were bridging. Pioneers. She said she had read my books so she knew that I had a young child, no health insurance, and a garbage bag taped to my bedroom wall to seal in a mold outbreak until I could afford to have it fixed. She even said that when I came over I could park in her driveway! A couple of weeks later, when I pulled my dented Hyundai Elantra up to the back bumper of her pristine jet-black Lexus, I felt like it was a symbol of the bond we were forging.

Over the next nine months we read books I loved at that age like *Bridge to Terabithia* and *I Am the Cheese* and *The Phantom Tollbooth*, as well as new books the girls or their moms recommended. We'd order pizza and the househelper lady would make a salad. We'd eat with our plates on our laps in the modern art plastic pillow room and no one got bent out of shape about using coasters. The girls were all adorable and smart and polite, and the moms were kind and respectful and complimentary about how I worked. It was a little strange going from mansion to mansion hearing about the other things in their lives, like Mandarin lessons and ballroom dancing and Paris again and fostering a baby elephant in Kenya and sailing underneath the Golden Gate Bridge repeatedly and yet another trip to the private screening room at Skywalker Studios, but not one thing about it pushed my "class issues" button in a negative way. They were classy and rich and incredibly privileged and they were cool.

The next year I got a call from a different mom wondering if I could facilitate a book club for third-grade girls. She said she wanted to interview me over the phone, which was fine, though she put me on hold for about ten minutes of the twenty-minute call. She was in finance. She was busy.

"Great," I said when it seemed like we had wrapped things up. "So, when did you want to schedule the first meeting?"

"Before I decide if this is a good fit, I'd like to meet you in person first," she said. "Can you come to my office this afternoon?"

"I'm sorry, but I have to pick up my son at preschool."

"Oh, you have a son? You're a mother? How are you going to make this work? Do you have child care? And you live in the East Bay? This sounds difficult. Well, I'd like to meet as soon as possible because I really want to get moving on this. And when you come in what I'd like to see from you is a résumé and a list of potential books for the first meeting with a synopsis of each book."

The minute I stepped into her office the next day, I could tell the receptionist hated working there. You know that look, like someone's been slowly grinding your face into the floor while hissing into your ear the exact insults that hurt you the worst as a kid. The receptionist had that look.

When she finally emerged (tight ponytail, tight face, tight clothes), I gave her the info she wanted, and after fifteen minutes of conversation I've blocked out because I was trying to please her and not really in my body, she decided to "try me out" for a session.

The night of our first book club meeting, a babysitter was on her way over while I sat on the toilet and simultaneously puked into the sink next to me. I called her and told her how violently ill I was.

"Beth, we are supposed to meet in less than an hour and you're just calling me?"

"I know. I just started feeling awful about twenty minutes ago."

"Well, I wish you could have given me more notice. It's going to be really hard to get a hold of everyone."

"I was hoping maybe it would pass, but I think I have food poisoning or something."

"This is going to be really hard to reschedule."

Jesus. I tried a different tack.

"I am vomiting and I have diarrhea. I mean, it's really bad."

"I don't need to hear the details, Beth."

When the next month came around, I over-communicated beforehand so that she would know I wasn't a flake. I had the girls read a book called *Year of the Panda* about a boy in China who adopts an orphaned panda.

I arrived at the giant colonial Laurel Heights home and the first thing I noticed was a heavy, formal vibe, even as I rang the doorbell. *Bing bong!* One of those doorbells that's made of real chimes. The househelp lady answered the door without making eye contact and offered to take my coat. She too had the face-in-the-carpet look. There was a round table set up in the corner of an enormous foyer that had a white tablecloth and purple place settings, a purple helium balloon tied to each chair, and purple goodie bags. Like a fancy girls' tea party. I peeked into the dining room. The long table was set in muted earth tones with potted orchids, two forks, plates and chargers, and stemware for water and wine. I honestly thought this must be set up for some event they were having the next day. Where was the pizza? I could hear the girls upstairs playing as the moms came out to greet me. They didn't look any different from the moms in the other group. Just very reserved. Cautious. Not warm.

I heard the main mom wander back in the dining room and say, "Well, I don't know. I guess she could sit in here with us. Or maybe she should sit with the girls. Is there even a place setting for her?"

It was decided it was easier to squeeze me in at the adult table. The chardonnay came out and the cook served an incredibly delicious Salvadoran meal with like five different components to it. I listened politely to the women around me.

"Oh, Hawaii was great," one said, "but I left my new Gucci sunglasses at the Four Seasons!"

Followed by: "You're kidding! We're going to the Four Seasons next week. Wouldn't that be great if I could just pick them up and bring them back for you! Let's call Rolf. He's the concierge, right?"

No one asked me anything about myself and I couldn't think of anything to say so I nodded along to conversations about Ski Week and husbands and teachers at the girls' school. My contact mom was clearly the alpha, but I didn't get the sense the other moms liked her very much.

Finally, it was decided we should move into the formal living room and get on with the book club. I was finally introduced to the girls; they were cute, but pretty young and shy. Only two of the moms had read the book, and they all sat on one side of the room in upright chairs looking cartoony, like the committee of judges from *Flashdance*, while the girls gathered close to me on the couch. I couldn't help but notice that the alpha mom's daughter didn't seem into what was happening. She sat close to me, hugging an enormous, expensive-looking stuffed panda her mother had bought her just for tonight. She sucked her thumb. Alpha Mom practically twitched with anxiety as the other girls chimed in about different endangered species or what they knew about China. Her daughter didn't say a word until she announced that she had to use the bathroom.

"You just went a few minutes ago," her mom said. "I want you to wait until the end of the discussion."

"But it's not me. It's for my panda," she said. "My panda has to go to the bathroom."

"Not now." her mom said.

"The ambulance is coming, Mommy. He's going to get on the panda ambulance now." And she took her bear and went upstairs.

The mom sat there, fighting the urge to go after her, but choosing to maintain her decorum. The night ended a little weirdly, the moms still seemed distant, but the girls were comfortable around me. That's all that matters, I thought. I could deal with the small army of tipsy power moms because the kids were sweet.

The next day I received a phone call. The mom thought, based on my performance last night, they would like one more trial session, but they would also like to renegotiate my fee. Each family would pay me ten dollars less per session.

"We all just thought you seemed a little green," she explained.

"I thought it went really well," I said. "The girls seemed to have a good time and I thought we talked about some interesting stuff."

"But this is the first time you've done this."

"Well, no. You got my name from the other group who recommended me."

"But it's your first time with this age group."

"Yes," I conceded. "I have never before led a book club for eight-year-olds. Only ten- and eleven-year-olds."

"It still seems very generous to me. The books aren't very long. And we're giving you an opportunity to get paid to learn a new skill. This could potentially be a very profitable business for you if you play your cards right."

It was true that I needed work. I always needed work.

"Plus," she went on, "you're getting the opportunity to be invited into our homes and have a wonderful meal served to you. That was a great dinner Lupe served last night, wasn't it?"

I told her I'd have to call her back. What a horrible piece of shit she was.

I called the friend of mine who has been in therapy longest and asked her what to do. Her advice was that I write a succinct email stating I would no longer be able to work with her. No excuses, no explanations. Her point was that this woman knows what she's doing and she shouldn't be rewarded with my participation in her lame negotiating strategy. I wrote the email, though I was twitching with dissatisfaction at not being able to tell her what I thought of her.

"You have nothing to gain from that," my friend said. "She wouldn't get it anyway. A person like that, it's not going to sink in."

The woman replied to my email saying she would only take five dollars off per family. I was enraged by the thought of these absurdly wealthy families saving thirty dollars a month between the six of them. I had to reply. Better than that, I had to Reply All!

"No," my friend counseled. "That what she wants. The power you have is in not giving her what she wants."

So I didn't respond. And I have held onto this stupid anger for years, this lack of closure on my part, this pathetic desire for a small revenge. But one good thing I did get out of it is a memorable phrase for when I need to honor the feeling in my gut and bail out of something I don't want to be doing. I thank that poor little girl and think, *I'm going to get on the panda ambulance now.*

Upstairs at the DNA

I WAS WORKING AT THE LOCAL INDEPENDENT WEEKLY doing ads for nightclubs and theaters. And by "doing ads" I just mean making sure all the performers names were spelled right and all the prices and times were correct. ("So you're sure the band is spelled Harry Pussy? Like it's a dude's name, not like a bush? Okay, and is the admission still three dollars or a canned good at the door?")

The main advertising guy at the paper was really into PRO-MOTIONS. PROMOTIONS were cool events you could do with the advertisers to make them like you better than their sales rep at the other weekly paper and ADD VALUE to the relationship. I got my first idea for a PROMOTION when I saw that Julia Sweeney was doing her one-woman show *God Said "HA!"* at a local theater. She had been on *Saturday Night Live*, right? Well, it just so happened that one of our other advertisers, a nightclub South of Market, was co-owned by another SNL alumnus, Rob Schneider. I approached my boss with this amazing idea. What if, after Julia's opening night performance, we threw an after-party at Rob's club and they both were there? We could ADD VALUE to our advertising relationships with a couple extra column inches of space, some deli trays, and a drink special, and make a happening out of it.

All parties agreed. I think Julia's manager told her that Rob wanted to host a party for her, while the nightclub manager was telling Rob that it would be a good night of business for him. The theater had four hundred seats, so if half the audience came, we'd have a successful event. Not to mention the crowds who would show up off the street when word got out that Julia *It's Pat!* Swee-ney and Rob *Down Periscope* Schneider were partying in the club.

When Julia's show was over, I rushed across town to make sure everything was ready for the party. I was a little concerned that it took me twenty-five minutes to get there and find parking, and for the first time, it dawned on me that the average theater-goer, no matter how much they adored Julia Sweeney, might not want to drive from the Marina to South of Market at 10 p.m. on a weeknight.

The club, one of those cavernous black boxes, was empty, which was okay. It was still early. A bartender directed me to a low-ceilinged room upstairs that was also painted black and had large mirrors plastered across two entire walls. It looked like a place you would do a lot of ecstasy and watch yourself dance for hours or a barre-less ballet studio for goths. Definitely a location where you would never dream of eating the sliced salami, whose bits of white fat glowed eerily under the blacklight. I checked in with my client. Rob hadn't been seen yet.

Two smartly dressed moms from the show finally wandered in, with their purses strapped diagonally across their bodies as they clutched onto them with both hands. They gave me an earful about how far the party was from the actual event and what a hell of a time they had parking in this terrible neighborhood, and when you enter the club there was no indication that this room was even up here, and now they weren't sure they wanted to stay. Patiently I listened as I watched the lights strobe across their faces. They were right. This was a garbage idea. If only I could stop Julia from coming.

Within a half hour, a handful of people arrived, and that's only if you're not counting the thumbs on your hands. Rob had been spotted earlier, but had bailed for other parts of the club when he got a load of the scene. And then Julia showed up. She was exhausted from performing, but put on a cheery face for about thirty seconds, until it dawned on her what was happening. The way her expression changed, as if it was her fault that no one had come, was devastating. She kindly chatted with a few people until the manager dragged Rob back in and here was my moment: they exchanged an awkward hello, Rob made a joke about how lame it was, and Julia laughed nervously.

I had orchestrated a night where two former TV stars said hello to each other in a dark room while nine people watched. To stand there and watch her, a woman I had just seen perform a beautiful monologue about losing her brother to cancer before going through cervical cancer herself, to see her standing around a dirty, loud nightclub trying to be gracious because some dumb twenty-six-year-old wanted to please her boss. I built that. I couldn't apologize enough.

Piece of Nirvana

KURT COBAIN LIT MY CIGARETTE ONCE at the Catalyst in Santa Cruz.

It's been about ten years since I said that sentence out loud. Once I realized that everybody I knew had heard me say it at least once, I finally stopped. Not that I trotted it out all the time, only when someone mentioned Kurt Cobain or Nirvana or the Catalyst or cigarettes, or sometimes Courtney Love. Have a celebrity anecdote that is more than one week old? Just stop saying it. See how it feels to abandon something you thought was precious that actually means nothing. Find out who you are when you can't dazzle the crowd with your "I had lunch at a table in between Celine Dion and Dianne Feinstein" or "Joe Montana brushed past my barstool and I think he said sorry." Those are just a couple classics from my personal vault.

So my boyfriend and I had seen Nirvana a few times. He was the kind of person who had *Bleach* on vinyl in '89. We were together for nearly five years and he still has an antique chair that belonged to my grandmother and has never returned a single one of my many calls asking what happened to it. I thought about placing one call to him every day until he responded, like this saxophonist I knew who was never paid a hundred bucks for a gig he played. He literally called the guy every single day for six months straight, every day, until the guy (okay, Stephan Jenkins from Third Eye Blind) finally sent him the check.

My boyfriend and I backpacked around Italy together after college, at the precise moment Nirvana was blowing up. We left the country before *Nevermind* was released, and when we returned "Smells Like Teen Spirit" was blaring out of every car and apartment and café and bar in San Francisco. It was my only experience of loving a band before they got big, and it made me feel conflicted and sad because I was twenty-two. They were opening for the Red Hot Chili Peppers at the Cow Palace on New Year's Eve? Even though that sounded like the last show on earth I'd ever want to go to, we were operating in some sort of panic mode. They were our band and now even my brother was listening to them, but we had to go to see them play because we always went to see them play.

When the night rolled around, we were having friends over for wine and spaghetti in our new dumpy apartment in the Mission. It became clear that we didn't want to go to a huge disgusting mess in an arena with all those frat boys. (What a simpler time it was when "frat boy" was the worst kind of human I could conjure!) The tickets were twenty dollars apiece, the highest price I'd ever paid to go see a band, so there was no choice but to get over there and sell them.

Kids were already puking in the parking lot when we arrived. Ignorant in the ways of ticket scalping, I rolled the Honda Accord into a spot and stood on its bumper, yelling up to the stadium lights, "I have two tickets to sell!" A crowd gathered quickly and the bidding war began. Forty, sixty, ninety. Before long it was up to a hundred for the pair. People were moving in on me and one drunk dude even tried to grab the tickets out of my hand. I jumped down, exhilarated, but unsure how far to take this. That was when my boyfriend pointed out one young teenager standing off to the side who had tried to buy them when we first got there, a half-wasted kid who could only offer face value. He stood there watching the spectacle, looking disgusted.

"Why don't we just sell them to him for what we bought them for?" my boyfriend said. "C'mon. It will totally make his night." I would love to say that this was my idea, or that I immediately agreed with him, but it wasn't and I didn't. I tried to protest, but because I am not made of stone I let my hot fantasy of being able to buy real Parmesan cheese and more wine for everybody who was waiting back at our house evaporate. I did, however, feel the need to demonstrate to the gathered masses what exactly was happening in front of them. I made a big deal about singling the half-wasted kid out in front of all the people who were waving their money in my face. Oh, how I loved my new role as salt of the earth hero! Doing the right thing, karmically and punk rockically.

I used to tell this story a lot, not as many times as the cigarette one, but still too many. Except I always made it sound like it was my idea.

Manners

I ALWAYS HUG YOU WHEN I SEE YOU. I say, "Hey! How are you doing? What's up? How have you been?" I pretend I don't know that you came to a party at my house one night and said to my friend that you'd never noticed before how much I resembled a newt.

Crime Scene

MOM'S OUT AT GENE'S GETTING ME POPSICLES BECAUSE I'm home sick with a sore throat and when she gets home, she is never going to believe this. She's going to freak out!!! I get up at the commercial, the 7-Up one with the song that always gets stuck in my head.

Feelin' 7-Up, I'm feeling 7-Up! Sharing styles and sharing smiles, I'm feeling 7-Up!

I go to the fridge and get the ketchup. I put a little on my wrists and my neck, not too much, and then I put the bottle back.

It's a crisp refreshing feeling! So crystal clear and light! America's feeling 7-Up and it sure feels right.

Then I lie down on the caramel-colored naugahyde sofa and I wait. I wait. I watch Andy Griffith climb into Barney Fife's sidecar and try not to smear the ketchup. Then there it is: the garage door opening. She's here!!! I position myself so that the top half of my body is slightly falling off the couch, but my legs are still on.

Like someone has come in and slashed me and then left.

Wait — they left? If they left, I should open the door like the slasher just escaped.

I jump up and slide open the glass door so the cold air blows in. Like the guy who does bad things slashed me and ran out. Hurry! Lie down again. Limp. Go limp. I try to be still, but my heart is pounding so hard you can probably see it coming through my pajama top.

Keys jangle, the rustle of grocery bags.

"Hi, honey!"

She's so cheery. Always. I think that's why she cries so easily when we give her cards from the drugstore.

How many grocery bags does she have? Did she get Pringles? Every time she shops she makes a joke about how she comes home with more than she went there for.

"Honey?" A little worried.

Footsteps.

Waiting, waiting.

A gasp! A scream!

Only then does it hit me. I have never heard her sound this way. Not on a roller coaster and not at a scary movie. I bolt up and run towards her, scared.

"I'm sorry, Mom!" The ketchup slides down my neck and hands, her face is frozen for a second, a mask. "I was just kidding!" I yell. "I thought it would be fun!"

She doesn't yell at me. She sits down next to me on the couch real close, puts her arms around me and takes a breath with her hand at her chest.

"Honey, you just have to imagine what it would be like if you came home and you saw me like that."

She brings me a washcloth to wipe off the ketchup and then she brings me a cherry popsicle. My favorite. I can't imagine her bloody and dead. She's too happy to die.

Piano as Pawn

AFTER FALLING IN LOVE WITH BRAD BOARDMAN IN fourth grade, I told my mom I wanted to take piano lessons. This was so I could ask Brad who his piano teacher was and then, having the same piano teacher, we would be one step closer to being boyfriend/girlfriend. Mrs. Packard came over once a week and I practiced every day straight for three months. As soon as I could play *Come Sail Away* by Styx proficiently, I dialed Brad Boardman's number, stretched the cord from the kitchen phone into the living room, secured the receiver by placing one of my mom's huge books about the Kennedys on it, and proceeded to play it for him the best I'd ever done. In return, Brad stretched his phone cord into his living room and played Styx's *Babe* for me. That weekend he asked me to "go around" with him at his sister's birthday party. I said yes and our romance was sealed. Then, with my mission accomplished, I quit the piano, never to play it again.

Game Plan

When asked to describe my parts you may as well
just say *part rugby scrum part military dress parade.*
Stay unshowered like Napoleon's love note and let the spindly
    hairs here and there remain in their coils within the flaky,
    scaly surface.
The opposite of *pliable* and *soft* is *fuck you, skull-licker, do you want
    to be touched.*
You do, which is a problem so top things off
with the cruddiest pair of period underwear
and a slouch that slouches deep into the most rugged slouchistan
and now you're ready for a night on the town.
Am I right, ladies?
The pile-up of non-ablutions when you step into this anti-
    groomatorium is one of your hurdles followed by more
    hurdles placed between this you and the future you who lays
    down at the finish line with her clothes off.
Soup to nuts is such a weird expression but soup to nuts.
Time is a circle masquerading as a writhing point entrenched
at two-thirty or five in the morning when you get in your truck
    knowing this is only one soggy and ineffectual piece of you
    carved
jigsaw-like, with a baby tooth from a cereal box.
Traffic lights go from red to green to yellow,
in the rearview you're never surprised to see
the easiest and most boring puzzle ever.

An Afternoon Date with My Stalker

THE MAN I KEPT SEEING AROUND AT THE poetry readings was old, perhaps even fifty. There used to be a small crew of them, post-beat stragglers who'd been here well before all of us, lurking around the bars talking about Ginsberg, Corso, and Ferlinghetti. Shabby and broke, they were specters of who we might become. And like most people I met who were over forty with terrible teeth and cowlicks, I figured this man had probably done something cool in life for which he had not been properly recognized. Gray-haired, narrow-shouldered, and pin-armed, it was like he'd never lifted anything heavier than a cigarette, syringe, or writing implement. He didn't sign up on the list to read and always stood in the back, bird-like, alone.

One night I had a big reading. I was only doing two poems, but the other people on the bill were Allen Ginsberg, Diane DiPrima and two older poets who had gone to the Naropa Institute of Disembodied Poetics. It would be obvious to everyone that I didn't deserve to be there and was only invited because they were trying to mix things up! with a young spoken-word lady who was going to recite a memorized rant about the fraudulent orthodontist she had as a teenager. Being the naïve comic relief "poet" was a role I was more or less comfortable with, but I was afraid of the audience. They would think I was a dilettante and an idiot. I went on first and remember nothing, except my tongue went to ash as soon as I spoke, and after it was over I sat in a corner, teeth chattering involuntarily for minutes. And then the skinny, intense, maybe-fifty-year-old I'd been seeing around came up and complimented me in a "cool guy" way. I believe he said Hey, I really dig your stuff. One of those compliments that's smoking a hand-rolled cigarette and wearing sunglasses. It meant a lot, though. Having the weathered scene veteran saying something nice. Who was he, though? Imagine when the only way to find out about someone was to suck it up and ask around.

No one seemed that thrilled by him, though I did find out that he had been one of the youngest writers to receive a Stegner writing fellowship from Stanford and was a long-distance runner, not just marathons but those endurance ultramarathons where you run a 100K or prove how far you can go in twenty-four hours. I also found out that he performed his poetry a few times a year in big venues, backed up with music by old jazz cats, dudes who had played with Cecil Taylor, the ROVA Saxophone Quartet, and Sun Ra.

During this time I was writing an online nightlife column under a pseudonym. I chose the extremely cool name "Mae Hemm" in order not to mix up this chatty blog with my "serious" writing. In the first few months, approximately thirty-five people read it each week. (Quite literally. My other job at the website was doing spreadsheets for the page view statistics.) At the end of the column, there was an email link to send in tips and gossip. Usually it was just bands asking if they could mail in their demo tapes, press kits, and CDs, but one day I got an email from the scruffy poet guy. He was recommending some upcoming readings and concerts and I was positive he had no idea it was me he was writing to. Only a couple of my friends were aware I wrote the column, and this guy wouldn't know where I worked. My name wasn't anywhere on the site. Over the next few months, he became a regular reader and would send an email almost every week saying he enjoyed something I'd written or giving me tips on what to write about. I liked having this online shadow relationship with a semi-famous local poet.

One morning I came in and there was an email from him, sent at 3 a.m. *Where were you last night?* I wrote something silly back from Mae's account, that I'd been home with a cup of tea, reading a book, and that I wasn't really out partying every night. His reply was immediate. *I thought you wanted me to meet you at the show you wrote about. It seemed like you were telling me to meet you.* I pulled up my column to see how he possibly could have thought I was embedding a secret message to him in my column. Nothing. Just a paragraph about a country-ish punk band from Austin. I wrote back asking what he was referring to. His reply: *That bar is right around the corner from my apartment and I thought you were telling me to meet you there.* I didn't write back.

Then the notes started. I would walk into a bar or café on an open mic night and the bartender would hand me a note that had been left by him earlier. So he did know it was me. There was nothing too alarming in the notes, except for the fact that he was always apologizing that he couldn't make it, in a way that assumed that I was expecting him to meet me.

I walked into work one morning and the office manager uttered a sentence no one had said to me before: "Beth, you received a personal fax in the middle of the night." I walked to my desk and when I swiveled my chair around, there was a long scroll of a fax, about three feet long. I unfurled it, and handwritten in tiny, tiny letters was a note from him. The time stamp was from a hotel in London where he was competing in a race. I glanced at the phrase "your cilia-like sensitivity" and rolled it back up and shoved it in a drawer.

A few days later, my desk phone rang. It was him, asking me out to lunch that afternoon. I suppose I did what any young woman with no boundaries, common sense, or experience does: I said, "Sure. I'll meet you out front at noon."

He pulled up in a real shitbox '80s Toyota Tercel, the same kind of car my high school boyfriend had driven, looking more disheveled than the last time I'd seen him a few months before. He was short, but had the seat way too far forward so the knobs of his knees were almost at the wheel.

"Where are we going?" I said as he took off down Van Ness toward the freeway. "I've only got like an hour. Desk job. But it's cool. It's nice to get a paycheck every two weeks and I even have health insurance even though I've never used it. And the people are really nice. I get to write that column and hey, how did you figure out that was me anyway?"

I was talking a lot. It's not just that I was nervous, though. Part of me really wanted him to find me funny and interesting. Like a sick little sliver of me wanted to reassure him that I was worthy of his extreme attention.

I relaxed a little as he headed toward the waterfront on Third Street and pulled up to an outpost restaurant/bar called the Mission Rock Resort. One of my favorite musicians, Mark Eitzel, had just written a song about it, and I'd never been there.

It was a gray day, cold, and the place was deserted. They weren't serving lunch.

"That's okay," I say. "I'll just have a Guinness." Everybody always said it was like drinking a loaf of bread, so that sounded filling.

He got a glass of water and we sat by the windows, looking across to Oakland. He was mellow, perhaps medicated, and entirely without a sense of humor. He conducted an interview with me about my life and how I came to write. As I spoke, I realized that my story was pretty boring. Regular middle-class girl from the San Jose suburbs goes to college, moves to the city, writes some poetry, works at an office job wearing bad cotton/poly blend clothes her mom gave her for Christmas. I think he was hoping I would be more the "passionate artist" type. I mean, I kind of wished I were too, but there were some incomplete Excel spreadsheets waiting for me back at work.

We drove in near silence through the soggy streets and I felt relieved it was over. The notes and the faxes would stop now. I was obviously a dud and there was zero chemistry between us. And then he leaned over the stick shift and kiss-attacked me. The eternal question: to break free or endure it! I chose to endure. Plus, I may have had a boring story, but at least I could prove I wasn't a bad kisser. Wait. What was I doing? His pupils had transformed into skinny laser beams.

I jumped out of the car, went into the bathroom and rinsed out my mouth. I was a disgusting person. I looked in the mirror, like people do in the movies, and vowed something or other. To be better. To be different. To not engage with creeps even if they were semi-important poets. To finish compiling the page view statistics before I got in trouble. I skulked over to my cubicle, hoping my boss didn't catch me in the rearview mirror she had on her computer monitor.

When I got off work, I walked all the way to my new boyfriend's house and told him about it.

"You shouldn't have gone out with him!" he laughed. "You just went out on a date with your own stalker!"

Oh, shit. That's exactly what I did.

I chose to deal with it in the least direct method possible and simply ignored his emails and phone calls for a few weeks until he sent one last message saying that it was his final attempt at communicating with me. But it wasn't.

One early evening, just after this final email, Eli and I were walking back to his place after getting some coffee. He lived in a huge storefront on Mission Street with one of those black metal accordion gates in front of it. As we approached the building, we noticed something strange. One of the homeless guys who usually sat out front selling things had a bunch of new inventory. Lined up across the entire length of the gate were the poet's record albums, at least five copies each of three or four different albums, all emblazoned with his face, staring out at us.

"How much do you want for these?" Eli asked.

We bought a couple, went inside, and put one on the turntable. After we climbed up in his homemade loft bed, I went on to suffer another, deeper humiliation. Not only had I kissed my own stalker, but the man who had taken an interest in me, a man I presumed was something of a badass, was producing some extremely fartitudinous work. Eli and I looked at each other, mouths hung open in between bouts of laughing our brains out. I had officially kissed a white poet who talk-sang about the injustices faced by his black, brown, yellow, and red brothers, a man who squawked like a chicken during an extended saxophone breakdown, and the person responsible for attempting to craft a sultry thirteen-minute exploration about this mysterious and complex creature called "Woman." I buried my face in the pillow and screamed. I'd been trying for weeks to do everything right with this new boyfriend and now I had blown my cover by showing him who I really was: an easy target, a gallivantrix, a girl who might crawl through the transom even though the door is unlocked.

This is Thirty

8 PM: FRIENDS START ARRIVING AT THE Peppermill Lounge in Daly City because there are no cool bars in San Francisco anymore. Even though it's going to be hard for people without cars to get here, it features cocktail waitresses in sexy outfits, dim lighting, mirrored walls, plenty of booths, and a sunken conversation pit with a roaring fire inside a bubbling pool of water.

9 PM: A lot of people showed up! I can't believe I found this genie outfit at Thrift Town this afternoon and it was only six dollars. I always wear things that I buy in thrift stores without washing them first! I'm such a free spirit!

10 PM: Whoa, the locals are showing up now. This late on a Sunday night? Hey, it's not just cemeteries and malls out here, there are some gangs, too. That's cool. They're just chillin' in those booths back there. Laughing at us. Time for another gimlet and more mozzarella sticks. People brought me presents even though I said no presents. Amazing!!!

11 PM: I got books and three gift certificates to Amoeba Records and some cool lipsticks and my new boyfriend Eli got me a 1950s Remington typewriter that is so beautiful!

MIDNIGHT: Hey, where are all my presents? Where is Carrie's purse? Where is that vintage Polaroid camera Eli brought to take pictures of everyone? The typewriter is even gone. Everything is gone.

Santa Barbara Showpiece

DEAR MARTIN,

It's me, the lady who used to crash in that little room at your place on Carl Street. I am forever indebted to you for your generosity during that period of some months in 1994 when I was looking for a permanent place to live. Okay, you're right, "looking" is probably too strong a word. I'll be honest and say I was more "waiting for the right situation to come along." You were handsome and let me know the door — the four-foot-tall door with the barn latch, the door that led to a cove under your staircase — was always open for me to stoop into and faceplant onto the futon at 2:30 a.m. Thanks again for that. Every itinerant spoken-word performer trying to get out of the commercial baking world should be so lucky.

I'm here to apologize for the couch thing. Your exquisite, museum-quality, vintage couch. I hardly ever sat on it because:

1) I always tried to make myself invisible or very, very small when I was in your home.
2) Most of the vintage couches I admired up to that point in my life were shredded and stained, one even had a nest in it, so I was afraid my very history would mess up its pristine upholstery.

Hold it. Why am I even calling this a couch? That's probably bothering you. It was a goddamned showpiece, Martin. You told me you bought it at an estate sale in Santa Barbara, which was a classy way to buy dead people's things that wasn't St. Vincent de Paul. You guessed it had been made in the late '50s or early '60s and it looked like it could have graced the living room of Rob and Laura Petrie on the *Dick Van Dyke Show*. It was a huge sectional that curved in a perfect half-circle and was upholstered in a rich butter-yellow fabric with miniature periwinkle starbursts, woven through with a shimmery gold thread.

When you had to move you called me up because it wouldn't fit in your new place and you remembered how much I loved it. You knew I was cheap and there was no such thing as Craigslist, so you offered it to me for a hundred dollars. A steal. There was one condition: You would, under no circumstances, assist in its delivery. That thing was a bear. If I could extract it from your Edwardian parlor, it was mine.

The last day of your lease came and your flat had been emptied of everything. Everything except It. I told you I was working on it. You knew what that meant so you got a friend, humped the thing into your moving truck, drove it over to my place, where you had to double park on one of the city's steepest hills, cursing me loudly as you unloaded it into the garage of my 22nd Street saltbox. A filthy garage packed full of tenants' junk, that special mix of tennis rackets, college textbooks, Teflon cookware, holiday decorations, love letters, broken chairs, and bicycle parts built up over twenty years of peripatetic renters. As you left you cursed more directly at me: *Fuck this. This is exactly what I didn't want to fucking do when I sold it to you and I have no fucking time for this.*

My head dropped down and slowly I walked back inside. You revved the U-Haul engine against the 31 percent grade, your girl-friend looking like Princess Diana in the middle of one of her leprosy missions as the garage door closed.

And so the couch sat, waiting for the day I would find the perfect oversize drawing room to put it in.

A few months later, we were Ellis Acted — evicted from our house so the landlord could pretend to move in when he was re-ally planning on remodeling and raising the rent for a new set of tenants. I transferred what little I owned to a temporary spot on 17th Street with no storage. I was determined not to let the couch (and the bicycle that I never rode) became part of the garage's permanent installation. Why did I write "determined"? Oh, Martin! I went back a few weeks later and there was a new padlock on the garage door. I left a message with my old roommate to get the landlord's number, but she had embarked on a new life in Mendocino trimming weed and attending massage school, so of course I never heard back. One afternoon I walked past and the house had been stripped to its studs, a stack of redwood bones in the fog.

I want you to know I punished myself. I went thirteen years with hand-me-downs and freebies until I felt like I could put out real money for a real couch, a fat brown thing from the Crate and Barrel outlet that has too many cushions and feels like it should be in front of a flat screen TV tuned to *Friends* in a McMansion.

It's ugly, Martin. I hate it.

Asshole

MY FRIEND RECENTLY TOLD ME THAT HER MOM said to her as a little girl, "Wipe and then look at the toilet paper. If there's something there, if it's not clean, get more toilet paper and wipe again until the toilet paper is clean."

I remember no such instructions. Wiping strategy was never a topic of conversation at my house. I learned to wipe my ass when I was around three or so and never thought much about it until more than fifteen years later.

I met this guy on the bus one afternoon. He was one of hundreds in my Art in America lecture class at college, but I'd definitely noticed him. Who wouldn't with that bulletproof 1970s Jeff Bridges *Thunderbolt and Lightfoot* vibe. I forget what we talked about during the ride, probably Diane Arbus or Nina Simone like everybody else, but I remember it being so warm outside that all the windows were open and everyone's hair was going crazy as we got bounced down the hill into town. Before he got off, he handed me a piece of paper with his phone number on it. I got to the landline I shared with five roommates and within hours we were kissing. Within days, we were having sex. So far I'd only slept with one other person, but what we were doing was working for both of us. Or so I thought. After class one day, he suggested that we take a shower before we got into bed.

Next level. Nice.

There were sweet, awkward transitions that had to do with how a person gets undressed in front of another while standing in a cramped wood-paneled bathroom waiting for the proper water temperature to materialize. Naked with feet on the fuzzy lavender bathmat. Kissing a bit while trying to make conversation.

I like your mole.

Thanks. I used to say it was a melted chocolate chip when I was a kid!

Oh, wait. Keep it sexy.

Yeah, I really like your moles, too.

Then jokes.

It was so hot when you said my name last time and I was kind of like, hey at least he said the right name!

Then his turn for "sexy."

Your last name sounds like Lipstick. Kind of.

Thank you?

We stepped into the shower and started kissing. And then he got a bar of soap. He lathered this soap between his palms and started aggressively lathering up my ass, soaping the buns. I'd seen that in a movie, bun-soaping, but then, working the crack. I'm not saying he didn't have an ass thing, maybe he did, but it was probably just the average ass thing most people have, which is more than is credited in polite society. But it felt like more than that. It dawned on me in that moment, as a young man's San Fernando Valley hands worked my asshole, not as a porn star might have, but more like an attentive hospice provider, that I truly had been neglecting the cleanliness of that region for my entire life. Sure, I wiped my ass with toilet paper. Sure, I used soap in the shower. Most of the time. (But everywhere?) I flashed on our previous encounters: The splaying of legs, the rearing back with complete abandon that is the sole domain of young people who don't realize they will never look better than this.

This man was trying to do right for me and for himself. And for all those who would come after. I could imagine how he must have psyched himself up for that moment. Obviously liked me enough to say: I can't go on like this. I need to do something about this situation. How can I make this work? I have a plan.

Ciao, Bella

I WENT TO ITALY WITH MY BOYFRIEND AFTER college. We bought one-way tickets with a plan to stay until we ran out of money. There are few guarantees when you've budgeted ten dollars a day in Europe, but agitation, constipation, and foot fungus are chief among them. Two and a half months in, we were done.

The day before we were to go home, I saw a flyer at the hostel in Florence. A family was looking for an English-speaking nanny for two months with the possibility of an extension if things worked out. I was broke, tired, and looking forward to being back home in time for Thanksgiving, but surrendering so easily gnawed at me. Maybe I shouldn't bail yet. Maybe the real adventure was just around the corner. *After* my boyfriend went home.

I called the number and a woman with a deep New York accent answered, but in Italian. *Pronto!* As easy as it is to make fun of people when they go to a restaurant and try to order their *melanzane parmigiana* and *orecchiette fagioli* in perfect Italiano, it is equally enjoyable when they don't try at all. Debbie from the Bronx got me up to speed pretty quick. She had traveled to Italy after high school, met her husband, had three kids, stayed. She was looking to hire someone because she was having surgery and would need help with cooking, cleaning, and the kids. I wanted so badly to ask what kind of surgery, because at twenty-one you don't know all the kinds of surgeries there even *are*, but I knew it wasn't polite. I would have to look at her and guess. A few hours later, she arrived at the hostel to bring me back to her house.

Debbie in her white Range Rover immediately reminded me

of some of the rich moms from where I'd grown up in the South Bay: blond hair, pretty, exhausted, secret smoker. The attractive children, between three and eight years old, sat silent and spotless in the backseat. We drove out of Florence and into the countryside, hills strung with grapevines, towering cypresses bending slightly in the breeze at dusk, and arrived at their home, a 17th-century stone villa that had been refurbished in an impeccable, rustic farmhouse style. I imagined afternoons of the children playing games in the fields, shopping at local markets, becoming a better cook, improving my Italian, and spending the evenings quietly with my books and journals. There wasn't much in my history to suggest that I was this kind of person at all, but the excitement came in thinking that maybe this was who I was meant to become.

The children disappeared upstairs to play, the older boy cheerfully carrying the younger one on his back, while Debbie went to make us espresso. Then her husband came home. When that man walked in the door, I had to consciously think about how to arrange my face to mask the thought that here was the most sexually attractive person I had ever seen up close, and he was looking at me at the exact same moment I was looking at him. He was tall and well-built, not too muscle-y, with a realistic bit of a dad-paunch. His dark skin looked perfect next to his white button-down shirt, and he had an open, easy smile. Eyes: caramel. Nose: Roman. When I think of him now, over twenty years later, what pops up first is where my eyes went when I averted them out of shyness. I see his forearm with a sleeve rolled up, hand still on the doorknob, bathed in light. His name was Maurizio.

The kids heard him come in and tromped down the stone staircase to greet him. They climbed on his back, kissed him all over his face, laughed and squealed as he wrestled with them. Debbie went to lie down and Maurizio told the kids to take me for a walk around the property. *Show the American girl that it's not so bad here.* We walked past smaller outbuildings and a vegetable garden, a vast green lawn, and a covered swimming pool. When we came back, Maurizio was setting the table with a huge bowl of pasta with mushrooms and greens and a fresh salad. I could still barely look him in the eye, but I liked to imagine his forearm at work. Stirring things, chopping things up.

As the kids excitedly tested out their English on me, Maurizio and Debbie exchanged a look. It was a look that made me think I'd gotten the job — though it's disingenuous for me not to admit that I'd had the thought that perhaps the job was that Debbie was actually dying and I was being auditioned for the role of the new wife.

After dinner we piled in the car, stopping for gelato on the way back to my hostel. *Stracciatelli* sounds so much better than chocolate chip and the kids told me they got ice cream every day. As we cheek-kissed our goodbyes and said *buona notte*, we agreed that I would call them from the hostel's pay phone the next day and talk specifics. It seemed like a done deal.

I entered the dark communal bedroom and went to my boyfriend's bunk. *I think I'm going to stay,* I whispered. He was silent, half-sleeping, though I know he heard me. Lying awake on my cot, I made a list of reasons it made sense to stay in Italy. I hadn't taken two years of Italian for nothing. If I didn't stay now, when would I come back? If I wanted to continue on my pastry chef career path, something I'd been working hard at for the past three years, I could study in Italy where, thanks to Catherine de Medici, many French pastries originated. Adventure. Opportunity. Finding out what was wrong with Debbie. Maurizio's forearm.

In the morning, as my boyfriend packed his bags, I made my case. As usual, I couldn't tell what he was thinking. We'd been together for two years at this point and were planning on getting an apartment together in San Francisco, but maybe this was it for us. If, after two months in Italy, I couldn't wait to get home to him, perhaps we were meant to be together. And if I didn't, who knows what could happen.

"If the job sucks," he said, "at least you'll be getting paid to live in one of the most beautiful places in the world."

His smile, his acceptance, his acknowledgment of my opportunity. That's what I wanted from him. We had spent nearly every minute of the last seventy-five days together in Foggia, Napoli, Ancona, Genova, Milano, Roma, Perugia, Siena, Torino, Bari, Savona, Bologna, and Venezia and I felt too connected to him to say goodbye. I grabbed my suitcase and threw everything into it. I left Italy without telling them where I went. I had no money for a phone call.

Tongue Rape

I WAS GETTING UP OFF THE COUCH a minute ago to microwave this leftover tofu scramble that is not as bad as it sounds, frankly, and even has bacon in it, when I thought of you again. I still can't figure out why this happens every few months. Surely there are more worthy candidates. Didn't I once make sushi with a nice redheaded boy from Vermont? I never think of him. Or how about that really cool lady with the famous astrologist brother who gave me a shiatsu massage on the beach? What was her name? She was fun. Haven't thought of her once in twenty years. But there you are, lurking, somehow permanently cached in the browser of my brain.

This took place back when I was fresh and exciting and apparently less guarded. Before the waiter forced himself on me after the restaurant Christmas party had moved to that guy's basement apartment. Before the time I found myself accidentally making out with my own stalker, which is never a good way to draw boundaries. But those times were different. Those times I was definitely asking for it. You're not even supposed to say that or tell impressionable young people or dicks in charge that it's a thing, *asking for it*. But I believe TOO LATE is real sometimes. I believe there's such a thing as shutting up and learning from your mistakes.

I'd spent a long day touring Vatican City and even enmeshed myself in the throng of thousands waiting for Pope John Paul II to make an appearance on some big old balcony. Once he stepped out, so tiny and shrouded and hunched, I was able to mill around for about five minutes of his indecipherable mumbling before I couldn't help myself. I had to leave to get another slice of pizza. To make it clear: I had already had a slice of pizza a half an hour before while walking, rushed, on my way to see the pope, but then the pope came out and all I wanted to do was say I saw the pope and then get another slice of pizza. And then I wandered back to my youth hostel and did what I usually did on youth hostel bunk beds: Lie on top of my sleeping bag, try not to touch the industrial plastic mattress cover, and wonder what I was going to be when I grew up.

Emerging out on the street again at about 6 p.m., the city was still warm and a little sleepy. There was a feeling that all sorts of things were going to transpire that evening, things I couldn't even begin to imagine. I felt very removed from these things. Italian boys, scooters, nightclubs, cigarettes, wine. These were for other people, or possibly a future version of me, but I couldn't see it. Gelato I could handle. I enjoyed that. I ate a lot of it. Recognizing it as ice cream, but more sophisticated, was key. This was the level I was operating on. More than ready to return from months in Italy having peak experiences with gelato and pizza and the pope.

When I first spotted you on the sidewalk, I smiled. You were like the adorable great-grandpa character in a movie, the silly one whose brain is full of holes. And you noticed me right away. How could you help it? My wardrobe strategy for the trip was a conceptual one. I would pack only items of bright, solid colors. Yellow shirt. Green skirt. Red pants. Orange sweatshirt. Pink cords. Blue sweater. I figured I could mix and match any of the items and they would obviously all go together in an amazing way. I looked like a toy that hangs off a stroller. My shoes, one of two pairs I brought, were purchased at a store in the mall that catered to geriatric travel. Seemed practical and my mom paid for them. Basically, it was kind of like I *was* my mom, but I was twenty-two. (Topic to explore later: Why do so many menopausal women dress like babies? Puff-paint sweatshirts, teddy bear sweaters, fun patterned socks, etc.)

When you looked up and said something to me, I was thrilled to get to use my Italian. I couldn't quite catch what you were saying, so I moved in closer, stooping down about six inches. You said it again, oddly more quiet this time. I liked that you were so old you didn't know English. It had grown tiresome, all those young Italians raining on my parade by answering my Italian with English. *Cosa?* I said. *Scusi, che cosa?* And as I looked into your pointy gnome face, with hair spilling forth Chia-pet-like from your nostrils and ears, a smile forming on your mostly toothless biscotti-hole, your hand reached out like a claw from the crypt, grabbed the back of my neck and you shoved your tongue into my mouth. Then you really went for it as I struggled to break free. How could you be so old and miniature and yet so strong? It's a comforting thing to keep in mind as I go on shrinking every day.

I guess I just want you to know that your tongue was gray and slimy and narrow and quick and rigid. I hate that you tricked me like that, by being eighty and whispering so softly in Italian. I think of you often. You must be dead now.

Assrace

This young fag called me up and told me he wanted to win the
    Assrace.
He said it like I should know what one was
Like it was a buffalo slider or Zumba or Tweeting
Or any of the words that have come along recently like
    microhood.
In order to win he needed me to tell him where Elijah Wood
would be before our interview
so he could position himself accordingly
holding a small flag trying to blend in with the crowd.
I was given a number to call
his ass would race over
so he could display it.
It has been called mooning for the past hundred years
Or pressed ham when it's up against a plate glass window at
    Denny's.
I looked into Elijah's blue eyes that night
And did not complete my assignment.
He probably would have liked a surprise ass
Who wouldn't.
In the end I voted for propriety over
bare asses on a red carpet
and will I ever forgive myself.

Sorry, Po

I WAS AT A DINNER THAT WAS CALLED a salon because all the people invited did something creative like write books or design restaurant interiors. Po Bronson, author of the number one *New York Times* best seller *What Should I Do with My Life?* and a man who was once named Sexiest Author Alive by *People* magazine ("intense blue eyes," "swing dancer"), was making a toast. He was making a toast for what seemed like a long time. Po's toast started out with a story set on a rooftop hotel bar in Los Angeles where he had been hanging out with a pal of his on the night of the Emmys. Some of us knew the friend of whom he spoke, a cool writer guy who had left San Francisco to join the staff of the anthropological forensics procedural *Bones*. Po went on about the man's other television and film projects in development and how he himself, Po, had been down there to take a few meetings, and how as they sat on the roof having drinks they realized: *We are so lucky. We have come a long way. We are doing it.* And how proud he was of his friend! And impressed with his bravery!

I did not doubt the sincerity of any of his statements and what I did in response was completely inexcusable. It just seemed so braggy and out of touch with most of us in the room, for whom twenty dollars for dinner felt like a splurge. He had been up there talking for twice as long as anyone else, and I just got impatient and jumpy and decided to follow my gut. I balled up my napkin and threw it at him. It unfurled softly against his chest and dropped to the floor. I took a quick inhale of breath.

To throw your napkin at another person while they are

speaking! As soon as I did it I knew that it was wrong and rude, and it unfortunately started a thing where a lot of people began throwing their napkins at him. I sat in half-delight, half-dread as at least a dozen were launched in his direction. In front of his wife who had just been so enthusiastic talking to me about the new customized cowboy boots she got in Austin and how her toddler loves The White Stripes.

I'm sorry, Po. I want you to know the temporary surrender of impulse control was such a blessed relief, though. Like I was shot through with a hailstorm. To feel like such a creature, an animal.

The Letter

I DIDN'T GET MAIL AT WORK. I WAS the assistant to the assistant to the publisher and every morning I would sort the bins of mail, noticing how every employee at the paper had a mail slot except for me. One afternoon I was sitting at my desk, stuffing envelopes and weathering another round of the closed-mouth burps my boss emitted like clouds from a factory smokestack on some sort of cryptic schedule, when my boyfriend, the office manager, came over and delivered an envelope. It was registered mail. I had to sign for it.

As far as mail goes, it was absolutely beautiful. Thick paper stock in a perfect square, deep red and shiny like a wet heart. I couldn't imagine who would be sending it, but it was already undeniably romantic. I pushed aside the hundreds of photocopies I'd just made of op-eds about the Hetch Hetchy reservoir and PG&E, noted the Massachusetts return address, and opened it. Inside there was a Polaroid of a pretty woman with brown curly hair, and on the bottom edge was written in Sharpie, "Follow the Golden Rule."

Mike's wife. She had found me.

Mike was someone I had met a few weeks before at a show at the Bottom of the Hill. He was in San Francisco making a record and we'd started talking. We went out for martinis at the Rite Spot the next night and met for lunch the day after that and then he went back home. He called me a few times and told me he thought he should finally leave his wife. Not because of me, he said, but also because he met me. It was incredibly sad to me. They had been together since college, nearly twenty years at this point, and when she found out she was pregnant, they talked it over and decided not to have it. He said they were never the same after that, that them deciding to not have a kid hadn't made them stronger as a couple, but felt like some kind of defeat. A resignation that it would always just be the two of them, but they weren't very happy.

This was pre-Internet and she must have worked to figure out how to contact me. Instead of writing her a letter of sympathy or apology, I was too disturbed about being contacted out of the blue when, at that point, I had done nothing wrong. I slipped the Polaroid back inside its red package, grabbed a manila envelope and copied the return address onto it, and put it into the outgoing mail bin.

Ghost in the Latrine

I STEPPED UP TO THE SINK IN A public restroom where a woman was having trouble getting the automatic faucet to recognize her presence and dispense water so she could wash her hands. She kept violently thrusting her hands forward and sighing loudly. A little more drama than seemed necessary, but I got it. I hate when those things don't work. The crazy dance you're forced to do. She switched over to the next sink and put her hands under the thing. That one didn't work either. Trying to be funny, I said, "Whoa. Maybe you're invisible!"

The woman whipped her head around and I could see tears in her eyes. She had already been crying. I started to say something like, I mean, they're so annoying! But she cut me off. "Oh, that's cute!" she railed. "You think a woman my age likes to be told she's invisible?!"

She was about sixty. Natural gray hair in a short bob. Purple cardigan.

I was so surprised by her reaction that my reflexes took over. The same thing happened that always does when a stranger yells at me in public: My eyebrows lifted and I chuckled lightly in her face.

"How can you be so rude?" she said, bewildered and upset. "What's wrong with you?"

I wanted to explain my joke, that we were all ghosts and the machines didn't recognize any of us. But I walked out instead.

Word on the Street

THERE USED TO BE A CREW OF HEAVY-DUTY weed smokers who lived across the street from me. They were usually pretty mellow, would just pull a few kitchen chairs out onto the sidewalk and drink forties and smoke blunts. Occasionally they'd have parties, but I'd only call the cops if they started doing donuts in the street or throwing firecrackers at each other. Or one time this guy yelled *motherfucking bitchass nigger punk!* on a constant loop until I couldn't take it anymore.

One night a video team from the Rachael Ray show came to our house. I was going to be on the show for my book and they were doing one of those "Subject Relaxes in Her Home Environment" montages where I was instructed to pretend to make dinner, pretend to read a book, pretend to put on makeup in a mirror, and pretend to play a board game with my son. Every stage of it was pretty awkward, but getting my six-year-old excited about a game of Yahtzee! only to cut it short after a few minutes was probably the worst. Look how happy Mom looks playing a game with you. I'm only pretending to have fun! Now I'm going to hug and a kiss you from a few different angles and tell you to get out of here and keep it down!

It was a pretty stripped-down group, but they had a pro lighting set and stayed for a few hours. When it was finally over, I walked them outside and the juice crew was still hanging across the street. They yelled something at me that I couldn't make out and I waved to them. That was about the extent of our relationship.

A few weeks later, I was outside talking to my neighbor

Nay Nay. I've written about Nay Nay before because she was one of the friendliest and most hilarious neighbors I've ever had. Everybody within a few blocks knew her, and her style of gossip was admirable. She'd couch her insider information in the form of advice or a warning. Like "Beth, you don't have to worry about Curtis coming around anymore because he ran off with somebody else while his wife was in the hospital after her stroke." Or "If you see a big dude hanging out with Kiki, it's her brother who's going to stay with her for a few weeks after he gets out of Lompoc for kidnapping, which he only did because they were his kids and their mama was on drugs."

So Nay Nay says to me, "What'd you have going on at your house the other week? We saw all the lights going on in there."

I told her the deal, which prompted my other neighbor Tony to say, "Oh man, I love Rachael Ray. She's real cute. When you see her, check out if you think she's thick or not. I used to watch her and she seemed real thick, but now it looks like she's lost weight or something. I like a thick girl."

"Well, tell you something," Nay Nay says, "they be talking about you from across the street."

"Oh yeah? What'd they say?"

Now it's Pee Wee's turn. Pee Wee sometimes hangs with the juice crew and used to drive a Pepsi truck until something happened that he won't talk about. "What do white people call it when they all have sex with one another?"

"Um, an orgy? Pee Wee, I'm pretty sure some black people go to orgies too." Most of my conversations with Pee Wee are about the differences between black people and white people, which we both greatly enjoy.

"No, that's not it." He thinks for a second and goes, "Swingers! They say ya'll are swingers!"

"What?" I break into a small prickle panic. "Who said that?"

Nay Nay jumps in. "Don't worry about it. They sitting there

smoking up and saying they saw you making porno movies in there."

"In my house? With my kid there? That's crazy!" I laugh extra hard for a moment until I realize that makes it look like I'm lying, so I stop abruptly, which also looks weird, so I start again.

"That's just what they saying," Pee Wee says. "They say they could see stuff going on."

I imagine a scene out of some French farce where the shadow-play makes it seem like a woman is performing a striptease when in fact she is sorting laundry and then holding two casaba melons next to a suspended salami. We did a couple takes of me climbing up a stepladder to get a book from the bookshelf. Could that look like something? Was our celebratory Yahtzee! dance too full of verve? When I did my "answering the front door" thing, did it look like I was expecting the pizza delivery guy?

I turn to Nay Nay. "Do you think I should go over there and tell them I wasn't? I mean, I don't want them thinking I'm making porn in my house."

She laughs. "They just smoking and making up stories."

"And telling everyone in the neighborhood," I add.

"Well, yeah," she says "but I always think the best thing to do is to not say anything. Rise above, Beth. Rise above."

I trust her so I don't say anything, but part of me thinks she didn't particularly want the story to die. I wonder if it's still part of her Prince Street lore.

Dog Towel

THERE IS A TIME IN YOUR LIFE WHEN you start becoming a guest in other people's homes. These people are seldom married, but are more likely a couple who is living together for the first time, which feels exotic because they don't have any housemates or anything. Like there is no guy named Craig or Domino renting the small storage room under the stairs playing Neil Young songs on the guitar at night when he can't sleep. Either that, the Neil Young songs, or just unrestrained, balls-out sobbing.

These couple-friends say to you, *Come up to Portland any time. We're renting a great little bungalow while Jody is getting her master's in Public Health.*

And no one has any babies yet. Babies are like phantom demons at this time in your life and you are sure that only the most boring and conventional among you will ever have them. Babies smell horrible and cramp your style. Babies are the ultimate paradox; born so that you can start to die. But these people, your friends, are well on their way to having one of their own. Therefore, the stench of death is fully hovering over Jody and Dave. They are about twenty-six or twenty-seven. Old.

How interesting the way some people live, you think, standing in their tiled foyer as you examine a coatrack featuring carved kokopellis, those little humpbacked Native American guys who play the flute. And look at the pristine bathroom with its blinding grout and bounty of clean towels folded on the freestanding rattan shelves. The towels are an explosion of primary colors. As if to make drying off a celebration. As if they're saying, *Hey, do you party? I heard you like to party.*

The cool water will feel good after a day spent on the interstate. Separate the folds of the shower curtain, a see-through vinyl one except for the parts where there is a colorful map of the world. Look at all that ocean hanging around and you've barely been anywhere.

After shutting off the shower, your eye moves to another stack of towels on the shelf below. These towels are grayish and beigeish and thinnish. There are about ten of them. A lot. Grab one of those instead. The humble ones.

But now smell your naked body. You used a quarter-size dollop of the Pink Grapefruit Body Wash, but somehow your skin reeks musty and barfy and you are matted with the short black hairs from Lucky. Lucky, who greeted your arrival today in the traditional snout-in-the-vagina style.

Later, when you are dressed, your friend brings you and the other five houseguests into the bathroom and gestures at the two stacks of towels. He is making a performance of it.

"All I'm saying is what kind of person looks at those two stacks of towels . . . and then uses *those?* Who among you would do that?"

Everyone laughs while you clamp your jaw down hard like you're biting off more of that buffalo jerky from the Winnemucca gas station.

"Those just looked like your nice towels so I didn't want to use them," you say.

"Yeah, they're our nice towels. They're the towels we put out for guests in our house," he says. "Towels for people."

Winnebago Master

IF YOU'RE SUPER MACHO ABOUT DRIVING THEN YOU wouldn't think twice about taking the wheel of a thirty-foot Winnebago in the middle of a snowstorm and driving it over the Siskiyou Mountains across the Oregon border even though it's a rental and you didn't tell them you were going out of state and you're not supposed to put chains on it, but you stop and get chains to be safe even though they don't fit the tires that well and then drive that motherfucker sixty miles per hour through the winding pass because you used to drive Highway 9 to Santa Cruz so you can drive anything fast. I wish everyone would wake up so they could see how amazing I am.

Beth Lisick is a writer and performer from the San Francisco Bay Area, currently residing in Brooklyn. Her books include the *New York Times* bestselling comic memoir *Everybody Into the Pool* and the gonzo self-help manifesto *Helping Me Help Myself*. Lisick has toured the U.S. and Europe as a solo spoken-word performer, front person for the band The Beth Lisick Ordeal, and member of the groundbreaking queer roadshow Sister Spit. Her other projects include comedic performance for the stage and screen with Tara Jepsen, curating the monthly Porchlight Storytelling Series with Arline Klatte, and teaching creative writing to young adults. She played the female lead in Frazer Bradshaw's award-winning feature film *Everything Strange and New* and recently received a grant from the Creative Work Foundation to write a book about the developmentally disabled artists at Creativity Explored in San Francisco.